Fully Human Fully Divine

Awakening to our Innate Beauty through Embracing our Humanity

Craig Holliday

Satori Sangha Press

Fully Human Fully Divine
Awakening to our Innate Beauty through Embracing our Humanity
Craig Holliday

Copyright © 2013 (Satori Sangha Press)

Satori Sangha
230 E. College Dr. Durango, CO 81301
Visit our website at **www.craigholliday.com**.

Disclaimer: This publication is designed to provide accurate and personal experience information in regard to the subject matter covered. It is sold with the understanding that the author, contributors, publisher are not engaged in rendering counseling or other professional services through this publication. If counseling advice or other expert assistance is required, the services of a competent professional person should be sought out.

Library of Congress Cataloging-in-Publication Data: 2013919782
Printed in the United States of America

Print ISBN 13:- 9780991130702
2013919782 Completed 29-OCT-13

Book Design by (**Wavecloud.com**)
Photos by
Editing by Emily Hartsfield & Jennifer Christensen

First Edition: October 2013

CONTENTS

Fully Human Fully Divine

For most of my life I've dreamed of being a monk and hiding out in a secluded monastery on a mountain top, far away from the insanity of this world—where I could simply rest undisturbed in the peace that comes from a life of meditation. If any of us look deep within ourselves, we may find that we too have a similar desire to experience a peace that has no end, to have a life free of chaos, filled with the never ending experience of Love. Intuitively we know that this inner peace and love exists, that is why we seek it through so many different avenues from religion and spirituality, from vacations, from relationships, from drugs to meditation retreats. For me this seeking came in the form of meditation retreats. I always felt that if I could disappear on some never-ending meditation retreat that my life would be perfect, because I would no longer experience the pain of being human.

For much of my life, I tried to get rid of myself—my humanity through spirituality. I've gone on countless meditation retreats, aiming to transcend this world and the suffering that comes with it. I've always loved these retreats and the bliss and peace that came with them, but they were never quite long enough and at the end of the week, I always went home to my old *self*—with all of my confusion and pain. I often found that I was a little kinder, a little more open and aware, yet I was never able to fully transcend myself and the suffering of this world. I was continually disappointed that at the end of the day that I was still *fully human*.

This practice of trying to transcend my very humanness and the experience of suffering went on and on for many years, until one day my teacher reminded me that *all of life is Divine.* Even though he had told me this hundreds of times in the past, this time I *heard* him. So for the first time while I was consciously on the path, instead of focusing on transcending myself and this world, I began becoming friendly with my humanness, with my wounds, pains, and neurotic sense of self. With this new attitude, I again began to practice with the intention of walking

1

toward those places that I wished did not exist. Instead of doing what I normally did, which was to try my hardest to escape life, escape my own mind and my very humanness, I focused on actually *loving the places that scared me*. I can vividly remember the first time I fully embraced my teacher's words and how my life changed dramatically when I shifted my attitude from seeking to escape, to *embracing all of Life as it is*. The power of his invitation became apparent on one retreat many years ago. In the cool fall air, tucked away in the mountains, my teacher guided us to become friendly with our humanity—to fearlessly embrace the dark places within us. Ironically, what I discovered through this experience of *embracing my pain* was our absolute *Beauty* and the *Beauty* of all Creation. How paradoxical it was, to discover overwhelming Beauty in our humanity and in the very experience of suffering—the very places that most of us are trying so hard to get rid of.

I realized I had been asleep to this mysterious ever-present Beauty my entire life, because I had been lost in the nightmare of my mind and was using spirituality to avoid this very nightmare. Yet fortunately on this particular retreat, I decided to do something different. I decided to embrace all the painful, sad and broken places within myself, instead of running from them. As I embraced what I thought was ugly within myself something unexpected happened—I *glimpsed* my true nature. From that quiet glimpse or moment of *Satori* something vast woke up in me, that many years later came into being. Through the ongoing practice of fearlessly embracing everything within, I discovered an indestructible essence and a supreme intimacy with the absolute goodness and Beauty of Life. This Beauty I speak of is not something we achieve from being good or honorable, it is our very nature; it is the very force that animates our being. This Beauty is the very quiet innocent presence that is reading this sentence right now. This book is an invitation to discover this absolute goodness as our very own self by embracing every aspect of ourselves........

The invitation of the Ineffable

What follows is a collection of reflections on what it means to be free and liberated in this world—through embracing the absolute Beauty of our Divinity and our *humanity*. It is an invitation to the conscious discovery that no aspect of our life is outside of the realm of the Divine. It is an exploration of how our very humanity is the doorway to our innate Beauty. It is an invitation to see that *all of Life* is Divine— from our struggles, pain and suffering to our bliss and vastness. This is not an invitation to solely experience spiritual freedom at the end of a ten day meditation retreat, but to be *Freedom Itself*, even while life is falling apart around you; while the kids are fighting, while experiencing heartache, while losing your job or place in life. This book is a doorway to our freedom, a freedom so vast that it includes every aspect of ourselves and our lives, even the parts that we wish did not exist.

What this book offers is both the *perspective* of what it actually means to be free in our practical dally lives and the *invitation* to join in this freedom in our *direct experience* of life. What this *practically* means is that we are able to feel and experience this freedom in our hearts, minds and souls—that we have the direct experience of being God in human form. In order to truly be free, beyond simply a mental understanding of freedom, we must *directly experience* ourselves as the *awake space of awareness* beyond our collective egoic conditioning that has been given to us by our past. This book is an invitation to step into the awake, aware space that is our very true nature and from this space, to then work with our habitual and repetitive minds so that we can maintain our freedom as everyday challenges and situations arise.

Yet in order for us to maintain our freedom, we must know how to work *skillfully* with the difficult aspects of ourselves, the places within us that we normally ignore, or hide from; because if we do not learn how to work with our *shadows,* we will never be free for any extended period of time. This is why throughout the majority of this book, I focus on and offer down to Earth practical teachings on *working with* pain, anxiety, and difficult emotions such as sadness, anger, heartache, as well as change, transitions, loss and our relationship to the experience of suffering in this world.

What follows is an invitation to courageously embrace our hopes, fears, sadness and pain, and to learn to uncompromisingly love every aspect of ourselves—and in doing so, becoming fearlessly free. It is the invitation to step out of our habitual and neurotic minds and into the beauty and vastness of the universe and to live *as* the very movement of this force here in our everyday human lives. It is an invitation to see that our life is perfect with all the difficulties and challenges. To discover that our life is the very essence of God in creation, and to discover that we have a choice to consciously join in the dynamic movement of evolution Itself, as awakened conscious beings here on Earth.

This invitation to the realization that *life is Divine and that we are the very embodiment of this Divinity here on Earth,* only becomes possible if we are first willing to put down our old belief systems about life. This requires that with humility, we question our collective egoic conditioning on every level within ourselves, as well as question our ancient spiritual beliefs about this world and our place here in it. For us to look deeply at ourselves and our world in an unbiased way, we must first become humble and empty of our assumptions that we have about life and ourselves. Furthermore, we have to be willing to examine everything within us, until we find the Beauty of our hearts and make this truth the object of our constant attention—until it is our very identity.

If we are going to know directly what it means to be free, to be awake, to be enlightened—we must start by investigating what we have been *taught* about enlightenment or spiritual freedom and our place here in the world—and how these two are intricately connected. For thousands of years religion and spirituality has taught us to deny ourselves and this world, and to seek enlightenment in transcendent states or to seek spiritual freedom in heaven, while denying our humanity and the overwhelming Beauty of this world. Yet if we follow a teaching about spiritual freedom which denies ourselves, which denies our humanity, which denies our world, we will miss the overwhelming Divinity that is overflowing from this world right here, right now. If we buy into the age old belief that we are here to *transcend* this world, simply to leave it behind, we miss the opportunity to live a divine life as fully enlightened beings sharing our unique purpose here on Earth. Instead of believing in this old belief that enlightenment is the end of the spiritual path, only to be found outside of Earthly life, we may instead choose to view enlightenment as a radical new beginning from which we *can choose to consciously evolve as the dynamic movement of Life Itself.* Because as long as we deny any aspect of ourselves with our hopes, dreams, fears and struggles, and simply attempt to bypass our fundamental humanity and our greater purpose here, we will only be deluding ourselves by trying to escape life through spirituality. If we choose to deny life through spirituality, our spiritual path is little more than another sophisticated egoic game of escaping.

There are simply too many teachings that emphasize denying and transcending the world, while missing the creative, dynamic, and evolving aspect of this Divinity that we are. I have met and studied with many individuals who have tried to simply transcend this world, to only later one day crash and burn, because they did not do their personal work. I was also, one of those individuals. As I started the path, I tried to transcend my suffering, and get rid of myself as quickly as I could as an attempt to find freedom; yet to only find 14 years later that, my humanity—my vulnerabilities, my pain and agony, my hopes and fears, along with my innocence and tenderness was the doorway into the very freedom, I had been searching for. With humility, what I have discovered is that with spiritual awakening there is no end, no ultimate resting place; this world, this Life, who and what we are is the vastness of the Universe, and the dynamic and continual growth and evolution of this Divinity as our own Self.

Many teachers say that this world is simply about awakening, and coming to the end point of nirvana where suffering ceases, where we become the *imperturbable stillness of mind*, where we realize our innate unborn perfection and simply rest as this perfection. While this is a humble and lofty goal, many of us may wonder what this means in relationship to our practical daily lives where change seems to happen on an hourly basis. Realizing *imperturbable stillness* as our true nature is absolutely necessary if we want to be free, yet discovering our unique purpose here, is also absolutely essential to the embodiment of this freedom. What I have discovered is that although spiritual awakening and the unimaginable Peace that comes with it is overwhelming profound, life changing and fully incredible; this is not the full story, but only half the truth. Awakening to our true nature of peace is not the end, but a wonderful new beginning; liberation is not the end of the path, but the pregnant ground out of which our fully conscious life begins. Would it make any sense that the purpose of the spiritual path and this world, was for us *to wake up out of it* and to come to some *ultimate resting place?* What would be the point? For our awakening and liberation to be complete, beyond the realization of our innate Divinity pregnant with all potential, we must also discover that we are the dynamic movement or force of the Divine here on Earth, right now in our mortal frames, right now in our busy lives. To realize this, we must come to the conscious choice *to be here* in this evolutionary world *as* the very movement of Evolution Itself. This book is about waking up to the discovery that we are both the static never changing, pregnant potential of the universe, *and* the dynamic, ever evolving expression of that potential. What this means is that we fully acknowledge our innate Divinity and Beauty as our Self, and that we consciously *choose* to grow and evolve as a dynamic expression of Life Itself in this world. In a humble and practical way, this means that we look at our life with an open heart and humbly and passionately walk *toward* the places within us that are still dark, still deluded, still suffering and bring the force of Love with us, as Us to heal, liberate, and transform these very places within us—for as long as we are human, we will still have these places within us because our lives are *the very matter of evolution.*

All the great sages and masters from Jesus, to the Buddha, to Ramana Maharshi, to Nisargatta, to Sri Aurobindo have reminded us that we must continually work with our humanity. As long as we are in human form (or any form), we will be growing because we live in an evolving universe. Because we are one with the Divine and the Divine is both the unmanifest and manifest, static and evolving, we too are both the unmanifest and the ever evolving manifest. In fact, awakening and liberation are steps in our very evolution. Although they *seem* from one perspective as if they are the end, as we realize our total Divinity and innate perfection, one day we will see that they too, were baby steps in the great span of things.

For the purposes of writing this book, I choose in a practical way to simply focus on working with our humanity, because this is where we all seem to get confused and struggle and this is also, the arena where we are ripe for growth. Our humanity is our evolving edge; it is the point at which our innate, unborn and undying Divinity meets our dynamic, unfolding, evolutionary Divinity. When I sat down to write this book, I chose to focus on the practical steps toward *spiritual awakening* and to not discuss the endless array of *spiritual experiences or byproducts* that come *with* awakening, (these two are often confused) so that the reader could simply focus on waking up to *what is here* in every moment beyond our collective egoic conditioning; and from this perspective of freedom, to then work with our humanity, so that it more accurately reflects the innate Beauty that we are. When our work is twofold in this way, we experience a total awakening: first to our unborn nature and next to our ever becoming nature. As we awaken to both, we become a dynamic individual operating from the vastness of Divinity in this world.

Acknowledgments

My work is based on my direct experience and on thousands of years of wisdom that has been passed down from Teacher to student. For the good part of twenty years, I have been on the receiving end of this wisdom and feel inspired to share what has been shared with me. I will not offer a teaching in the form of an intellectual philosophy or dogma, but rather an *energetic transmission* that comes from two sources, which are really one. This transmission comes from what I have received from Life and discovered in myself, as my Self and what I have been given from my Teachers which have I tried, put to test and found within myself. It has been my commitment to myself and to my Teachers, that I will not offer anything in this book that I have not found within myself to be true.

From one perspective, it may seem as if I plagiarized this book. The teachings contained in it belong to my Teachers and their Teachers and ultimately to God, Life, Reality or whatever we call it. Many of the teachings that I have received, I have written them down word for word as best as I can remember them. This wisdom does not belong to me. It belongs to my Teachers and it has been gathered from teachings on countless retreats, workshops, meetings and through my intimate work with them. My main teacher David, I must fully thank and acknowledge for he has taught and apprenticed me for almost 20 years now; to him I owe the deepest acknowledgment, he has been my constant guiding light and has modeled *total mastery* to me. And yet, he wishes to live a mostly anonymous life outside the chatter of the modern spiritual world. I have to humbly admit that the wisdom I have received from my Teachers is on each page of this book. I hope this is clear and that the credit goes to my teachers: Life, David, Adyashanti, Ammachi, Jon Bernie, Andrew Cohen, Pema Chodron, Kehaulani, Byron Katie, Lama Tsultrim, Eli Jaxon Bear, and Matt Kahn. Also I must thank my kids Amaya, and Noah, my mother and father, my team of editors, especially

Emily Hartsfield, Jennifer Christensen, and Kathleen Grady, my friends and family for all their support. I must also thank, all those I have had the honor to study with, and to those who have broken my heart wide open; to them I bow again and again. I ask for forgiveness from anyone who I have not acknowledged. Furthermore, if I misquoted or did not acknowledge anyone for teachings contained in this book please forgive me. Any teachings I share in this work or in the meetings that I offer, I have first taken deep into my heart, found their Truth and put it thoroughly to use, and have allowed the teaching to become my direct experience, until it is no longer separate from me. Often through this process, I have forgotten the original source of much of this wisdom; for those unacknowledged teachings, forgive me.

Becoming Intimate with Surrender

About six years ago, I was given the opportunity to become intimate with what it means to *truly surrender* to Reality. This was not brought about by any effort or doing of my own, but came as the result of my totally failing at life. At that time, I was at the end of a divorce, remodeling my house, starting a new business, living with chronic and intense back pain, going to graduate school, working for my Teacher and trying to raise two kids. I was living in a state of anxiety, despair and overwhelming stress. I had just got off the phone with my ex-wife, who told me that she had happily moved on and was coming to pick up the kids and they were all going to float down the river with her new boyfriend. At that time, I was exhausting my egoic will trying to keep everything in my life together—yet Life had a different plan and my egoic consciousness cracked under the pressure of it all.

As my ex-wife pulled up to my house to pick up the kids, I was in the midst of pouring my daughter a glass of pink lemonade, and my body began to tremble out of control. I dropped the glass and then the pitcher, as my kids quickly walked out the door to go have some fun. Uncontrollably, I fell to my knees and began to wail, as I realized that I could not hold my life together any longer. I fell backwards on the cold tile floor, and the spilled lemonade dripped off the table and onto me. I laid down in a puddle of sticky lemonade and my tears. I sobbed and wailed, and let out a cry from my gut, "I surrender God, You win. I surrender, You show me the way." Instantly, I was met with the feeling of an absolute and unconditional Love that filled my entire being. This love filled and overflowed from my being as I cried, trembled and shook, while my heart broke wide open releasing layer after layer of the pain I had been carrying for so many years.

This overwhelming experience of crying and wailing went on for hours, until something paradoxical happened. In an instant, my emotion shifted from incredible sadness to uncontrollable happiness. I let out the most wild laughter as my tears drenched my shirt, as slobber drooled out of my mouth, and mucus ran down my nose. My belly ached and I pulled muscles from the violent laughter and cries that came out of me. I laid there in this absolute mess and sobbed and wailed and laughed for what must have been four hours, as my pain emptied out of me by the grace of letting go. With a voice hoarse from wailing and laughing, I continued to cry, "You win. You are the boss, I surrender to You," over and over again, as waves of anxiety and panic left my body, leaving me absolutely *spellbound.*

At some point, after gagging on my own mucus and drool, I rolled over and allowed the slobber to pour out of my mouth onto the floor and I realized that I was in *Heaven.* When I was able to sit up, I took off my drenched shirt and walked toward the bathroom to clean myself up. As I got up, I realized that I was completely disoriented. I felt as if a spacious halo of light had entered the space that I knew to be my mind and my body was overflowing with Bliss. As my eyes scanned the room, I directly experienced that there were no longer any walls or division separating me from the rest of life; it was as if my consciousness was everywhere all at once. I did not feel that I was in any way limited to my body, my mind or emotions, and at the same time, I felt totally physically and emotionally spent and paradoxically, like I was reborn into a new body and felt absolute oneness with everything. Up until that moment, I had never felt so wonderful in my life. My consciousness was as vast as the sky. I was spellbound by the ineffable Beauty of all of Life. Everywhere my eyes gazed radiated with such vibrancy and Beauty and this same Beauty was overflowing out of my heart. As I walked into the bathroom and looked in the mirror, I realized that this was the *first time*, I had ever really seen myself and what I saw was absolute *Divine Beauty*. I laughed, like a madman, because I also looked like a total wreck. I stared deep into my eyes and saw the whole universe. I stared at my hands and fell in love with their amazing vibrancy and aliveness. I felt like an angel had just incarnated into this incredible form. I took a few minutes to clean myself up and walked outside, stood in the middle of the street and fell in love with the absolute beauty of it all; it was as if the entire world had been reborn and was vibrating with Beauty and Divinity. I wandered around my neighborhood aimlessly for hours, in total awe of this world. Ineffable....

Later that evening, my egoic pain, began to gently come back into my awareness, yet I knew that I would never fully be able to believe in it again, and despite this pain coming forward again within me, my vision was unchanged. I was experiencing this great paradox of being a human and Divine. This book is about waking up to our absolute Divinity—to the absolute Beauty of Life, and never believing in our habitual and conditioned egoic minds again and living *as* this Divinity here on earth as an ordinary human in an ordinary life, yet in alignment with the dynamic force of creation as our very own Self. This is the invitation of the Ineffable.

About this book:

Sometime later I sat down and began to write about this seemingly never ending awakening. After six years, I had to stop myself from writing and began to edit this first book. I realized that I had written enough material for two or three books. This first book will be an investigation in the *most simple way* of what spiritual awakening is. What I have discovered is that until we are free of our conditioned minds, we will be lost in this world and at the mercy of our self created suffering. Although there are countless awakenings, beyond nondual awakening, this first book will focus almost completely on waking up to our true nature and living as This. What I have found is that this initial series of awakenings, which takes place in our head, heart and gut, radically changes our orientation toward life, and yet, is the *beginning* of the spiritual path, and is in no way the end of the story. This book is about waking up to the undivided discover of Divinity as oneself, and working with our humanity, so that there is little gap between our inner realization and our outer life. It is important to note that this gap will never fully be closed, because our ever evolving innate Divinity will always be a step ahead of our humanity. In this work, I will focus almost exclusively on this series of initial awakenings *in a practical, down to earth way,* and the embodiment of these awakening and their profound impact on our lives. My later books will contain the more mystical aspects of this awakening and the many awakenings that happen beyond knowing who we truly are. Feel free to question, to test and discover if what I say can actually be true..........

As you read this book, it may seem that I am the teacher, the one who knows in some *mental* way, it is not the case—I have simply reflected upon my direct experience of Reality. Life is the author and teacher of everything. I am the reader and I write this book to you and I write this book to me. I write to the one who wants to know, who wants to experience the Beauty of Life directly as themselves. I see no difference between the author and the reader. We are the same. The truth in me, in this book, if there is any, does not belong to me. Truth belongs to the source of all things. As humans we have minds and egos, and our minds and egos distort reality. They create projections and see the world through a lens of the past. Each time I sit down to write, I do my best to write from beyond the conditioned lens of my past. As you read I would ask the reader to do the same and drop all lenses, all projections, all separation. Join me in the undivided truth and vision of who we are.

Throughout this book, I will constantly invite us to awaken out of our own personal and petty nonsense, which is the cause of our suffering and into this huge nondual Reality—where source and actor are one. I invite you and me, there is no difference. The awake, alive awareness in you is the same awake, alive awareness in me. The ego in you is the ego in me. The invitation is constant for us, whether we are fully awake, or go in and out of the awakened perspective or just starting down the spiritual path or fully in the grips of egoic consciousness. The invitation is the same for us wherever we are, even if we are living as a fully liberated being—our embodiment and our human expression of our innate divinity can continually be improved upon, infinitely. Evolution has no end.

It may seem that as I write this that I think I know something. I do not. What I think I know is simply my *thoughts* and reflections pointing in the direction of freedom and should never be mistaken for the direct experience of Truth. What I directly know is my experience. For some reason, I have been gifted with incredible Teachers who have patiently worked with me over the years. I must deeply bow to my root Teacher David, whom I have had the good fortune to live and work in incredible intimacy with him for over half of my life. During this time, my Teachers have opened incredible worlds for me. Worlds so beautiful that if I described them, I don't imagine anyone would believe me, unless they had been there themselves. At times, it may seem like I know who and what my Teachers are. I do know them, from being in their huge presence; and at the same time, I have no idea who they are, for they are lifetimes beyond me in depth, wisdom and understanding. Why I was graced with their presence, I cannot say. In this life I have been a child, a charlatan, a liar, and a thief. By some Grace or Divine mistake, this fool was given the opportunity of a lifetime of Divinity in their presence. This opportunity awakened me into what I am now, which is still childlike in comparison.

After years of intense spiritual practice, study, seeking and failing miserably at life, something miraculous happened—this incredible Divinity began to wake up in me and in an effort to understand this experience, I write. This book is my exploration. My experience is continually and exponentially changing and growing, such is the nature of Divinity. Yet beyond this experience of myself is something huge, constant, unborn and yet dynamic. I do my best to allow this place to write through me and to keep my egoic personality out of it. Yet, this book is based on my experience. I write this not to add to my pride, but because I want to share with those who, like me, have been pushed and dragged out into the vast unknown by Life. My teachers have trained me to use myself as an example and so I can only directly write from the experience of myself. As you read, you may think that I am a fool, or enlightened, or not enlightened, or an egomaniac; all are true and none are true at the same time. My words are only pointers, pointing to the Ineffable.

I write this book in an effort to examine what it means to be free, to be awake, to be enlightened, to have no self, no ego, and as a practice to begin to have my inner realization reflected in my outer life. My Teacher has clearly showed me over many years what a Master Enlightened Being is. If you want to know what mastery is, find a master; I am simply a kid writing about the Ineffable. If you want to examine with me, what it means to be awake and how to work with a huge amount of karma and egoic conditioning—read on. If you want to examine what life before, during and after awakening is; what enlightenment is beyond ancient mythological or a dogmatic understandings—read on. If you are compelled to examine with me, what it means to be human and Divine—not in some philosophical sense, but in the context of a down to earth awakened practicality, join me in this. Through the years, I have been gifted with access to so many incredible sources of wisdom, studied with amazing Teachers, been on countless retreats, but none of it meant anything until I discovered who

I was at the depth of my being. After discovering this, I noticed that there is so much confusion in the modern spiritual landscape about what it actually means to be free outside of a dogmatic or religious framework. Not until recently, has there been much clear examination of what it actually means to be awake in daily life, with a wife or husband, kids, a job, and in our fast paced world with countless demands. The majority of the writings on the topic of spiritual awakening have been written within the context of the monastery, not much has been written on what it *actually* means to be free within the context of the demanding and high speed world we live in.

In our modern age, this truth seems to be making a huge presence outside of the religious traditions. It is becoming more and more apparent that all truths are available to everyone. With this comes the danger that it can be watered down. Yet this does not have to be the case for us. If we have access to truth directly, then it is us whose projection has the power to water the truth down. I invite us not to take this course, but to instead, allow the Truth we hear wake up the Truth in us. This is our invitation and in this invitation lies our Freedom.

The Space from which we investigate:

At some point along my long journey into spiritually, about 14 years into the Master/student relationship, I woke up to the discovery that *we are all God*. My initial awakening was brilliant, terrible, confusing, messy, and all over the place. When I say woke up, I mean there was a dramatic shift in my perspective of who and what I knew myself to be and who and what I knew the world to be. The shift was out of egoic consciousness and into something beyond words. I began to experience life as if I was a thief, a joker and God, and the trees, the sky, the mountains, everyone, and none of this and everything at the same time. I sat down and wrote while my experience unfolded, as an attempt to understand this awakening and as an invitation for others to join me in being who we are—for others to join me in what we have always already been, awake, alive, aware presence. Join me in this Beauty, and if you are already here, I too will join you to in the Ineffable.

Sometimes this book will seem like a bunch of nonsense or a doorway to the hugeness of what we are. Sometimes it will be a manual of what to do, or exactly what not to do. You are welcome to laugh at me, to argue, to question. But it is an invitation to go beyond skepticism of what is possible, to go beyond our collective, conditioned egoic mind, to go beyond our emotions, and yet to examine our conditioned minds and emotions—not from an egoic mentality, but from directly inquiring into the nature of things. This is our invitation, this is the context of this book, not to be some mental exercise, but to be something ground shaking to our minds, to our sense of self, to our egos, to our identity.

As you read, you may find that much of what I speak about is being repeated over and over. I did this because the nature of our ego is habitual and repetitive, and if left to its habitual nature it will quickly forget what we have just learned and will go back to repeating itself again and again. To wake up, we may need to be reminded countless times. I know my Teachers have spent years, and in some cases decades, saying these same things to me over and over again. It is not that any of this is radically new information, but what is powerful about this work is that within it lies a constant and never ending invitation. So do not read this book to try to get something from it, but rather take it as a doorway *to let go into* and if you happen to open up to this vast expanse and then find yourself again lost in ego, our invitation is to again surrender to the dharma. As we do this work again and again, we may discover one day that we no longer fall asleep—instead, we step into an opening as big as the sky, and everything forever changes, let that day be today.

The style:

When speaking about that which is Ineffable words simply break down, which means I will miss the mark again and again. To make up for this, I can only play with words and hope they come close. It should be noted that I use capitals in a way to invite the reader to see the difference between the words *beauty* and *Beauty*. The latter signifies Divine Beauty. I wrote in this way as a way to invite the reader to step into something beyond. Although I also, fully understand that all of life is Divine without exception; yet in my writing, I often use the transition from lower case to upper case to signify a shift in perspective. I did this purposefully throughout the book. Sometimes I have been inconsistent in this style, to break up any rigidity on my part and to remind the reader that all of life is Divine, by doing this I made my editor somewhat upset because I was breaking the rules of continuity. But I have always been someone who has had a really difficult time with rules, boxes and any type of rigidity. In regards to the use of the words *mind* or *ego*, I am referring to *our habitual and conditioned neurotic minds or egos.* Not to the healthy form of our mind and ego. I must acknowledge that we do of course, have wonderful, spontaneous, intelligent and clear thoughts that arise from our innate wisdom; yet because this is not a struggle for us, I will not spend much time referring to this healthy aspect of self when I use the words *mind* or *ego*. When I speak about awakening *out of mind*, I am not speaking about awakening out of our healthy wise mind or out of our psychologically healthy ego, I am referring to awakening out of our conditioned, self serving, neurotic, repetitive dysfunctional minds or egos. In addition, I tend to use the words *Life, Reality, God, Universe*, interchangeably also to break up any rigidity. That being said, as you read—please feel free to let go of any egoic rigidity or mentality and join me in the direct experience of this invitation to discover what we are……

What exactly is Enlightenment, Freedom and Awakening?

There are many different and confusing definitions of the terms awake, awakening, enlightenment, and liberation. Because of this it is very important that we take some time in the beginning to offer a basic definition of what awakening is—and this definition is simply a beginning, a pointer toward something indefinable and inexpressible. For the purposes of our investigation, we will start with a basic definition from which we will build upon for the rest of this book and hopefully our life. It can be tremendously confusing to develop an *experiential* understanding, if we are not clear about what we mean when we use these words; there are countless paths and traditions that speak about awakening in so many different ways and in the last few years the word has become so watered down and used in so many different ways, that I'm never quite sure what people mean by it. In my life, in my experience—after a lifetime of struggling and about 2 decades of studying and inquiring and being in close relationships with teachers of Enlightenment—I have formed a deep experiential relationship, with what it means to actually be free, to be awake; right here, right now in this lifetime. This direct experience is what I am inspired to explore. **The most basic definition of awakening is that awakening is a fundamental shift in identity out of our personal, separate and egoic conditioning and into Awake, Spacious, Luminous, Ineffable Awareness as who and what we are.** Years ago, when I first heard these words from my teacher Adyashanti, it stopped me dead in my tracks. It ended so much confusion about what awakening actually was and what I was left with was a direct experience of *Alive simplicity*, a simplicity that I had been craving for years. This simplicity is totally ordinary and yet, as vast as the sky. It includes everything and is the great nothingness at the same time. It is beyond any thought, concept, experience or perspective; and because it is always arising or existing in the present moment, it continues to be totally ground shaking to our everyday sense of self and leaves us immobilized by an incredible Beauty and intimacy that we see and experience in everyone and everything. This door that my Teachers have opened changed my life forever. Because once the door opens, it is like waking a sleeping lion, and as this lion wakes up to itself, our days of egoic identification are numbered as we begin to come home to the Beauty and Divinity that we are, right here in our mortal frames. As we wake up to our inherent Divinity, we realize that we are Divine, that everyone and everything is Divine, and that we are and always have been the dynamic vibrancy of Life itself.

Yet, awakening cannot be summed up in some brief definition; it has to be experienced and lived. After 20 years of intense spiritual practice, I am still contemplating, and discovering what it means to be awake in the world, and I struggle to put into words, that which is beyond words and understanding. That being said, throughout this book and my teachings, I constantly add to, contradict and build upon this understanding; because the deepest truths are paradoxical, ever evolving and expanding. Our collective egoic minds want truth to fit into a simple definition, or a neat little box; but the Truth that I am speaking of does not fit within a box, within a religion, or in this book. Truth is much larger than a definition, than a book and cannot be contained by any walls or boundaries. This Truth is beyond the play of opposites, and includes the hugeness of Life, includes the incredible complexity and simplicity of the totality of Life. This Truth is opposed to nothing and includes everything. Some speak about *one truth*, as opposed to some other religious or mental perspective of truth. I have no desire to speak in a way that divides our world into true and false. Our world, Life itself is paradoxically, *terribly wonderful*, and to live in Truth is to be awake, beyond the play of opposites of our minds or mental constructs. This book is an invitation to step into this Reality.

Throughout this book, I may use the words Awake, God, Life, Truth synonymously. To me it is all one movement of ever expanding embodiment of our True nature, yet along the path *awakening* is a significant shift into an incredibly new way of being, beyond our mental and emotional identities. And within this awakening journey there are many significant, subtle and paradoxical layers of awakening; and as we begin to wake up out of our insanity, our life which was once painfully confusing to us, finally begins to make sense. Not from some egoic or mental perspective of knowing how and why life is the way it is; but it makes sense because we wake up to Life, in us, as Us, and not until then will life ever fully make sense.

When we wake up, we are struck by the totality and complete oneness of our experience, of ourselves. As we walk through this doorway, we will feel as if we have finally made it home and have realized the Truth of who and what we are. While stepping into this for the first time, we will *feel* as if we have finally arrived and will experience an incredible completeness and *assume* we are at the end of our journey; but we are not. This tends to be the case, because our experience of awakening, by its very nature will always *feel so total*, that we may mistakenly believe that we have reached the end or have the total and complete truth. Yet to fully come into our embodied awakening, and experience a total liberation, we will experience, not one awakening, but a *series* of profound awakenings over a period of many years or even decades, despite how each individual awakening *feels*.

Paradoxically, each time we awaken to a deeper level or layer of ourselves, it is marked by an experience of totality, completeness and a feeling of finality and of ultimately coming home. At first, it will *seem* that we have finally made it home and can finally rest in our fully liberated embodiment; yet the process of awakening is ever expanding and includes the hugeness of the ever evolving dynamic universe—it has no end. A common example of this is when we wake up out of our conditioned minds for the first time, and we experience a vast, transcendental freedom beyond our thinking minds. Yet, a deeper, more inclusive and intimate experience of awakening, than this initial transcendent awakening is when our transcendent awakening descends into our hearts and we wake up on the level of our humanity. As we give ourselves over to this process of awakening, we will find ourselves awakening in deeper and more inclusive ways. This occurs as our emotional identity shifts from a place of being conditioned and unconscious, to a place that is more fully inclusive of a deeper level of our own innate Divinity, while simultaneously embracing our humanity and the beauty and pain and suffering of the world. This is the difference between being awake to *your* divinity on a mountain top compared to being awake to *everyone's* Divinity while in the market place. It is easy for most of us to have a transcendent awakening after being on a long retreat and during this time, we may feel total and complete and at one with our true nature; but does our perspective last? A much deeper awakening is when we can actually maintain our awakened vision when we come home from our retreat to our friends and families who may or may not have been happy that we were gone.

Throughout these pages, I will explore and attempt to define *awakening* in various contexts and forms and then add to these definitions, contradict them, destroy them, resurrect them, build on them and let them go. Remember these are just words, symbols on a page, and because of that, they will never be the thing itself; this book is a mere pointer to something ineffable. When we begin to inquire into what it means to live beyond our mental and conditioned perspective— when we begin to question who and what we are, a wonderful and beautiful transformation happens—we begin to actually wake up, and this is the invitation of this book, of this life. These words will never be able to adequately define this huge Mystery that we are, but they can point in the direction of it. If we open to the direction, to Life itself, we may begin to directly experience awakening to who we are beyond personality and ego, right here and right now. All it takes is a sincere *willingness* to again know who we are, who we have always been, beyond the movement of our conditioned minds.

When most of us think about who and what we are, we habitually look to our conditioned ego—or the movement of thoughts, emotions, and memories—to define ourselves. Yet when we are awake our identity is not found in our conditioned sense of self. Our identity is found in Alive, Awake Awareness as who and what we are. From one perspective we are already this. It would be impossible for us to not be awake, because we are all alive, awake awareness. Yet, the majority of humanity is lost in the endless drama of their minds and because of this, miss this incredibly obvious Divine Reality that we are. We are all walking around in God's hand looking for God, like a fish we don't even notice the water we are swimming in. But if we take a closer look, we find that it would be impossible to read this if we were not awake awareness. If we were not aware, we could not see or hear or feel. If we were not beyond our minds, we would not be able to reflect on them. We *are* aware *all the time*. For us to directly experience the significance of this, we must be present to *Awareness waking up to itself* in an alive and vibrant way.

Remember this has nothing to do with some intellectual insight or understanding; that is the world of our thinking mind and ego. When we know and understand from our mentality it is helpful, but not nearly as deeply powerful. What I am speaking about is ground shaking to our sense of self. When we wake up to ourselves, we wake up to the world of Reality. We see what is actually here, not what we *think* and *feel* about what we think and feel is present. This is quite different. Awake Awareness simply sees things as they truly are, and through this simple seeing we are liberated from the ever fabricated and constant complexity of ego. Freedom comes from being one thing, just *seeing*; whereas our egoic identity comes from commenting on, and analyzing, and thinking about, and processing and arguing. The ego's complexity is exhausting, while Awareness is simple and ever replenishing. Our freedom is in this simplicity, which *allows* for everything, and *is* everything at the same time, paradoxically.

The ego is a complex movement of psychological forces; it always thinks in terms of itself, and is constantly defending, upholding, and separating itself from life, even if it doesn't have to. The very function of the ego is to individuate or separate itself from the rest of life, and it approaches the quest for enlightenment the same way. It wants to have a spiritual experience of enlightenment and then attach an identity to it and show the world, how wonderful or different it is, in comparison to all others. Unfortunately for our egoic self, *our ego* does not wake up. This would be impossible. Ego is a habitual, conditioned movement of mind and psychological forces. Yet, most of us fully identify with this movement of mind as our self and have no idea that we have a choice to live beyond it. As we become conscious of this choice, we move in the direction of our own freedom.

Yet when we identify with this movement of mind, we suffer. We suffer because the mind is never truly satisfied; it never fully puts down its defenses to simply rest. If it did, it would cease to exist and we would be free of its chatter and chaos. But most of us never stop following the habitual and conditioned nature of our mind and this is why we suffer. But if we look deeply, we find there is something here that is beyond our suffering—that is beyond the psychological forces of our ego. There is something here *that witnesses* this whole dance of mind. When we believe in the movements of our mind and mistake these movements to be us, we experience limitation and separation. Yet when we know that what we are is *that which is aware* of and beyond this dance of mind, and begin to directly experience ourselves as that Awareness Itself, we experience oneness, unity, and expansiveness as our very own self.

Notice that nowhere have I said that the ego is bad and awareness is good. Nor do I say that we need to go to war with ego or get rid of it. Ego is an organizing device. It takes in sensory input from this world and tries to make sense out of it and protect us from physical or emotional harm. In a sense, our ego is like a protective and sometimes, practical mask we wear on top of our true self which is vast, luminous awareness. Without this mask, we would not be able to operate in the world in a functional way. When we first come into this world as babies, our consciousness is simply *oneness consciousness*, it is vast undifferentiated awareness. This is why newborn babies cannot tell that they are separate from others or their environment, because their experience of life is that of oneness and unity. This is wonderful for them as they lie in their crib and experience oneness with life, but not practical because the baby simply lies there in this state of unity with life, yet unable to function practically in this world or protect itself from harm. Without the emergence of an ego into our consciousness, we would never individuate or grow beyond the state of *oneness consciousness* that we came in with as a new born. Evolution has given us this gift of ego, so that we can have an individuated sense of self, which is necessary or we would still be lying in our crib waiting for someone to feed us. An egoic sense of self is a necessary mask to wear, so that we will individuate in this world, grow and take care of ourselves. Without an egoic sense of self, we may never know ourselves to be separate from our crib; we may never grow or eat or bathe or run from harm. Inherently there is nothing wrong with our egoic nature, it has its function to individuate from our environment, to protect us and help us to organize our experiences of this world. Yet after we have fully individuated and matured, if we want to be free to live beyond these movements of psychological forces, we must not mistake the mask that we wear, for who we are under the mask.

After we have fully individuated and matured in our sense of self, our ego only becomes a problem when it becomes our *entire* identity. Yet developmentally it is necessary for us to totally egoically individuate from our inherent oneness conscious that we are, so that we can have the experience of being human. A two year is supposed to believe in her egoic mind, and believe she is the center of the universe. Doing so helps her to separate herself from her blanket and her parents. In a sense if we never individuated, we would never be able to learn, grow or evolve; we would remain lying in our crib with a consciousness vast and free like the sky, yet unchanging, and our human birth would be meaningless and without the opportunity for growth and evolution. During this period from about age two to our early adulthood, it is fully appropriate for us to identify with our ego. Yet after early adulthood, it no longer becomes necessary for us to believe wholeheartedly in our ego as who and what we are, because we have reached a point when developmentally, we are fully individuated. At this time, if we have a healthy identity and live in a safe environment, we can put down our *egoic sense of self* and simply have a *sense of self*. Yet we cannot let go of our ego until our healthy development is complete, to do so often leads to mental illness is one form or another, because our egoic identity helps us to organize our experience of the world in a practical way.

I am often asked how or when the ego fully emerges in our consciousness. It does in two ways, first gently and gradually over a lifetime as it develops into its full mature expression; this is shown in our normal egoic growth through the stages of development from being a baby to being an adult. Also, the *trance of ego* emerges all at once into our consciousness as we first begin to mistaken the movement of our mind for our *self* through the experience of being shocked by the wildness of life. By this I mean that the ego fully emerges as our identity, at some point in our early development, when we experienced an *overwhelming experience*. When we experience intense experiences, our minds become over stimulated and as a result, we have an overwhelming stream of thoughts and emotions. To manage and organize this overwhelming experience of thoughts and emotions, our ego comes forward to create a sense of *operability* for our self, and to control and protect our self from harm. As this experience of overwhelming thoughts and feelings unfolds, and the egoic defense system that arises in response to them, we will inevitably mistake this thought and feeling steam and accompanying egoic psychological forces *to be who we are*.

For example, at some point while we were young we may have experienced something frightening, terrible or painful and became scared. Perhaps someone such as an older brother came and tried to take our blanket away and began pinching us and so our mind came forward to attempt to protect us. As a result our egoic consciousness emerged into our consciousness in an effort to defend and assert ourselves, and it began to try to hyper protect ourselves from others. We may have responded by pushing back or trying to hold on tightly. As this psychological force came forward in our consciousness, we began to fully believe in this defensive mask as who and what we were. It was practical and *developmentally appropriate* and easy to make this mistake in a moment of pain, because our ego may have been the only thing protecting us from harm. In these first initial shocking moments of our early life perhaps before we could even speak, when life scared or threatened or excited us, our ego became the *loudest voice within us* (it did so to get our attention) and as it did get our full attention, we began misidentifying this movement of our mind as our actual identity. This is *the trance of ego*. It arises as we hyper indentify with our minds, because we then hyper separate from Reality, thus creating our egoic self. This egoic self is a radically different experience than the experience of our natural oneness or inherent Divinity that we experienced as a baby and which continues to live underneath our mask of ego. As a result of this shift into our egos as our identities, we were able to individuate and also we experienced suffering, which comes from our false identification with our egoic mind as our self. We suffer because ultimately the trance of ego is not who we are, it is simply a mask, and *intuitively* we know this. This knowing that we are more than our mask, makes us feel empty when we identify fully with the mask. The good news is we can also shift out of this false identification with the skillful means of wisdom and compassion.

This dance of false identification can be easily seen in individuals who have experienced great pain; they tend to be hyper defensive, because their ego became scared or over stimulated and now reacts in a hyper sensitive way to life. There is often a correlation between the pain that we have experienced, and our reactivity of toward life. It is not that we should not be hyper sensitive in a moment of pain, this may be wise, yet what happens is that our ego often, continues to be hyper reactive to the rest of life after the pain or situation has ended. This is why if we grew up in war zone or unsafe environment, we may have more egoic defenses than an individual who grew up in a loving and stable environment. This is why it is essential for the healing of our ego, to first experience a loving stable environment. When we do this it will help create the conditions for our ego to relax enough to allow our defenses to drop and begin to trust and to surrender to a life that is beyond ego. When we grow up in a difficult environment our ego does not trust in the goodness of life. Yet at some point, if we want to be free, we must realize that our egoic defense system may not paint a clear picture of reality, and we must be willing to trust that there is another way to live.

To awaken, we must realize in the depth of our being that life is Divine, and that we can allow our defenses to drop, and that it is possible *and actually preferable* to live without defenses. To awaken means we essentially realize that we have a choice about how to live and make the choice to live beyond our ego—beyond a defensive orientation toward life. When we realize this, we see that we are not our egos. We are not our minds. We are not our emotions. We are that which witnesses the comings and goings of our minds and that which has the power to choose to act from our hearts. This is not a mental realization. If it were, it would just be another egoic thought. When we wake up, it is not like drinking a cup of coffee and having a sense of clarity; this is not what I am speaking about. When we wake up, we allow the foundation of our mind to fall to pieces; and our sense of identity crumbles as we step into the vast space of Awareness, while allowing our overflowing Divinity to embody us. We go from being limited and meeting life from one small perspective of a particular ego, to having *no* perspective and being intimate with everything all at once. Imagine being in an argument and intensely arguing your perspective; this is egoic consciousness. Now imagine the same situation and all of the sudden you no longer believe in what you are saying, or what the other person is saying, and you fully accept each other's arguments. Your perspective so radically shifts that, there is no difference between you and them, the floor and the sky, and all of life. It is beyond what the mind can imagine.

When I speak about awakening, it is not a light matter. It is as if God's vision and our vision become one. When one has an initial shift in perspective, it may be just a glimpse or it may feel total and complete; it may last for a second or never end. What comes is really not up to us, for awakening happens *to* us, it is not something that our ego does; in a sense freedom awakens to itself. Once awakening occurs, it may feel that we could never go back into egoic consciousness again and yet 99% of us will. Ego has a strong pull back to itself. Awakening is very much like the balance of riding a bike; as we ride we are carried by something mysterious, something beyond our thoughts or controlling nature. But as soon as we put our feet down, we are in the world of ego again. We can go back and forth between being awake and being asleep for moments, days, months or lifetimes if we choose to continue to believe in the constant drama of our mind as ourselves. But if we want to stay awake, we give ourselves to awakening and allow it to consume us— until we can no longer believe in the movement of the mind as who and what we are.

During the transition period from egoic to awakened consciousness (which could be decades), our egos may try to claim awakening for it self. Our egos will want to latch onto this experience and say, *"yes this is it, I am awake, I am superior, I am the enlightened one."* This is what egos do; they take something and make an identity out of it. Whatever comes through our experience, our ego tries to build another identity out of it. This is actually one of the most significant processes of ego, to constantly build identities—and awakening or enlightenment can be one of the most revered identities for our ego to attain. Yet true Awakening is not an egoic identity—it is the absence of identity. It is not something that we can hold. It is our very nature, the ineffable aware space from which everything arises, whereas the ego is just a movement, a program running within us, layered on top of our beautiful, spacious, awake awareness that we are.

If we go back to the bike metaphor, awakening is more like a verb than a noun. As soon as we try to put our feet down and say, *yes this is me*; we again become identified with our ego. In a sense, our egos are continually reasserting themselves and self fabricating an identity which creates the illusion of a fixed permanent self or a *me*. This identity is the fundamental illusion that sages have been speaking about for thousands of years. As our ego creates a self based on past experiences and conditioning, and projects this image onto the screen of our awareness, we mistakenly believe that we are this fabricated image. Our ego constantly recreates itself in each moment *out of habit*, and as we believe in this habitual movement, we become deluded into thinking we are something that we are not. It does this to constantly create an identity as a way to fabricate a self over and over again in whatever form it can, even a spiritual form. As it does, it creates the illusion of a solid self, but in reality it is simply a fabricated self. When we sit in meditation, we can watch this very dance arise before us.

Awareness on the other hand, does not need to create an identity; it is that which sees this whole dance and has always been here silently witnessing, the drama of our mind unfold. At some point while we were young, we believed in our *fabricated self*, and as a result, experienced ourselves as separate from the rest of life and with this separation came suffering. Yet when we step out of this dance of ego, we become free. And we stay free as long as we are not believing in our *self image* as us. Yet this becomes difficult because, our ego can create a self in a millisecond and does so continually. This is why it is called the false self; it is self fabricated, instead of being self existent Awareness, which is what we are. This projection of our mind is very much like a movie that is constantly running; we have been watching it so long that we have completely identified with it. The delusion is that we think our thoughts, the images on our screen are real and assume they are us, but they are not. Awakening is when we begin to see life directly; and get up, leave the movie theatre, and no longer believe in the projection of our minds.

The dance of going back and forth between *awareness being awake to itself*, and not being awake, but being unconscious is confusing because we can wake up to our true nature and yet, still experience a large degree of egoic delusion. Egoic conditioning does not necessarily disappear when we wake up. Often with awakening, large parts of our egoic conditioning fall away at once, but rarely does the whole thing disappear. In our spiritual mythology, there is this myth that we have a moment of enlightenment and our entire ego and all of our pain falls away as we float away on a cloud to our heavenly abode. The key word here is "myth." Some individuals, who have very strong egos, can have the experience of waking up, while much of their egoic conditioning remains in place. For the 99% of us who this is the case, we will continue to work to let go of our nonsense, our conditioning, and our habitual nature so that our humanity begins to reflect the beauty of our inherent Divinity. To be awake means we wake up to our Beauty, and see our nonsense very clearly. In this clarity, we can choose who to be: the fabricated self that continues living unconsciously or to embody our true self and live as our Beauty, our Innocence, and be free. As we consistently choose our Divinity, and we stabilize in our True Self, a bizarre thing happens—our ego begins to dissolve. After years of this process of our ego dissolving, it ceases to arise any longer in a neurotic or selfish and self centered way. A very practical small degree of our essential ego does remain, so that we can function in a healthy way in the world. But our whole orientation to life radically changes as a huge degree of our ego is released out of us. As we journey through this impersonal process, what we find is that the various conflicting and competing egoic voices dissolve and we are left with only one voice within us, the voice of the Divine as we are reunited with the Divine will as our own ordinary Self.

I don't like to use the word *enlightenment* much, because it signifies some static place. Some teachers use the words enlightenment and awakening interchangeably. I like to reserve the term enlightenment for the spiritual greats: Jesus, the Buddha, Ramakrishana, Krishnamurti, and for my Teachers who I have known and been graced with over long periods of time: David, Adyashanti, Ammachi, and Jon Bernie. I reserve this term for those who are Masters, those whose outward expression and inner Divinity match. Yet this whole idea that enlightenment is a place that we get to, is simply that— an idea. Our language does not accurately have words for what enlightenment is—which is more like a movement than a place we arrive or experience we attain. When one is totally aligned with Divinity in their inner and outer expression, we would not call that a place, or a static realization or achievement. We cannot say we have achieved Enlightenment; that would be silly, only our ego would want to claim this. This is why words and language break down, when trying to define or understand what Enlightenment is. Enlightenment is beyond words and definitions. It is a *movement*, an embodiment of Divinity.

Yet even if we do not fully embody or demonstrate our inner Divinity in our outward life, we are still fully Divine in our nature or our essence. But often we forget this, and this is the primary cause of our suffering. All of us are animated by Life, which is inherently good and beautiful. It is compassionate to remember this: *All of us here are expressions of the Divine, in a human form.* To awaken means to wake up to our Divinity, and to wake up out of our bondage to our egoic sense of self. As we awaken, we see the mind for what it is. We see thoughts as just thoughts, with no inherent reality. To do this, we do not have to be a saint, have good karma or be perfect. We simply have to slow down, become mindful the space of awareness that we are and see clearly that our ego is a *trance of identity*. Anyone can awaken from this trance of ego—a criminal or a sage. There is a spiritual myth that we must be holy or perfect, or a really good person to wake up to our True nature, yet it is not true. Everyone, because we are all Divine, because we all have and are Awareness, has the ability to wake up out of our habitual and conditioned nature and can know ourselves as that which is Aware. Anyone can realize that they are the one who is aware, instead of being the one who is identified with the contents of their minds. We all have this ability, to know who we are beyond our egoic or fabricated sense of self. This is what it means to be awake. Yet to be Enlightened, to be a master, our actions must match our vision and our inner brilliant Divinity; they become inseparable. This is the difference between being awake and being Enlightened.

I have watched in amazement, my own teacher David for 18+ years display an absolute mastery, and have been humorously waiting for him to not be in alignment with his Divinity. I have seen little mistakes here and there, minor human misunderstandings and confusion. Yet overall, he has been overwhelmingly amazing in his expression and embodiment of Divinity. Imagine being in close company with someone for 18 years and you can't even form an argument of anything they ever did which was out of alignment with their Divinity. This is mastery. Enlightenment *is* mastery and it does not come from will power or ego; it comes from total surrender to God or Life or whatever you want to call it. When we surrender this deeply, we become liberated. Our liberation, our total freedom comes when we surrender 100% and become slaves to the Divine movement. How terribly ironic this is; our egoic nature does not want anything to do with this type of freedom. The freedom I am speaking about has nothing to do with doing whatever we want—this is the freedom of the ego. Spiritual freedom comes from surrendering our ego, to the movement of Life in us, as Us.

Awakening is, in a sense, the beginning of the path to true freedom. It is often spoken about like it is the end of the path; but life becomes so new and rich after awakening that it really is another beginning. It is another birth in this lifetime. In my own search, I spent at least 14 years intensely seeking, visiting every enlightened teacher possible, meditating for hours every single day, working for my Teacher, traveling to India and going on every retreat possible. But all of this ended, when I discovered that what I was looking for, was the very thing looking out of my eyes. It had nothing to do with the *me* who I thought I was for so many years. This awakening did not manifest as a *new me* in the form of a polished, sensitive spiritual ego, wearing a robe and having flowing hair. It came in the realization that Life and I are one, with a dramatic shift in who and what I knew myself to be. It came with many added experiences, byproducts, and shifts in consciousness such as overwhelming bliss, incredible intimacy with all of life, explosions of energy throughout my body, a never ending array of spiritual experiences, the loss of my much of memory or past, Kundalini awakening, the dissolution of my will, cosmic consciousness, and experiences of spaciousness and expansion. What I learned was that the whole time while I was on the "path," I was chasing many of these byproducts or symptoms of awakening, of freedom. These 14 years, I was chasing experiences. But awakening, I learned, is not an experience, all experiences come and go. Yet, what we are cannot come and go. Awakening is the direct recognition of who and what we are: awake, alive awareness—and who we are not: our mind, ego, emotions, and body.

So in a deep sense, when I first woke up, it was a realization of what I am. Not an experience, but rather, a shift in perspective out of the mind or ego as me and into something much more unlimited. When I discovered this, the seeking was over. I knew from the depth of my being that I was not separate from Life Itself. Yet, I was gifted with a strong ego and a huge karmic weight. So this shift, even though powerful, was not in any way total and complete. It *felt* total and complete for some time, but when the byproducts of tremendous bliss and expansion began to settle down and integrate into myself as a normal part of my consciousness, I was faced with my same confused and disillusioned egoic self. Yet, I realized that I could no longer take my ego to be the truth of me. I was awake to who I am, yet at the same time flailing all over the place, in relationship to my conditioned self and others. I began to learn that I had a lot of work to do to begin to close the gap between what I realized and the expression of it in everyday life.

This gap can be tremendously confusing for most of us. We may wake up and know ourselves to be Awareness, and yet still be confused by our egoic conditioning and false sense of self. This is why I find it necessary to make the distinction between awakening and enlightenment. When I first woke up, I was not at the end of the path, but rather at a wonderful new beginning. I would use caution with anyone who says, "I am enlightened, I am at the end of the spiritual path" or anyone who speaks of any absolute finality. There is no end to our evolution while in our human form. Our form is always changing and evolving. We can never arrive at the end, because our expression of our Divinity is delivered through our body, mind, and ego. This outward expression takes place in an evolutionary body and mind, in an evolutionary world, so there is no end to the extent of our awakened, embodied Divinity.

What I noticed about myself after my initial awakening is that I had a lot of ego, which came as a shock—especially after experiencing an incredible depth of Beauty as myself and feeling as large as the sky. I had believed in the myth that our ego disappears with awakening. At first this myth was reinforced by my experience of cosmic consciousness. What often initially happens is that we wake up and out of our being, into our transcendent nature, and into the formless freedom and expanse of the sky. When we first awaken out of ourselves, out of our ego, we awaken into the realm of the transcendent, which feels egoless. This can last for a moment, a day, a year or even lifetimes.

Yet at some point, we come back down to earth and Life presents us with the opportunity for our awakening to *include* the rest of our being or to *deny* our humanity. If we make the choice to deny our humanity, we become detached, dissociated and out of touch from the practical reality of life. We will become totally unbalanced in relationship to the world and forced to live on the edge of society or in a monastery or convent. This was common in the past, yet in this age our challenge and invitation is to include everything—all of life. If we do choose to include all of our self, our transcendent awakening will come down into our body. As it does, we rediscover the pain of our egoic sense of self and being in a body. Historically, awakening out of our selves and into the transcendent, has been the end of the path in many of the ancient wisdom traditions. But the natural evolution of consciousness is to be inclusive and in this way, the movement of awakening descends from the transcendent realms and includes all of life, not just the transcendent. If we just hang out in the transcendent realms, nothing really changes; we just learn how to escape this world in a really wonderful way. It can be a beautiful escape, but in the end most of us will not be satisfied with stopping here.

So here again, awakening can be paradoxical. We can be awake to our True nature, and still have a big ego. If we reidentify with ego, at any moment, then we go unconscious again. Yet after awakening, it is difficult to go unconscious for too long, because we have seen through the illusion of ego. And once we see through illusion, we can never *fully* believe in it again. From one perspective, ego is a repetitive and habitual psychological force which keeps us repeating the same behaviors over and over again. As we identify with our thoughts and behaviors, our ego creates a solid sense of self. Yet awakening is the opposite of this repetitive psychological force—it is spontaneous, free, mysterious and impersonal. Once we step into this incredible freedom, it is hard to *fully* believe in the dream of our minds ever again and difficult to resist the pull of the Divine into Herself.

This initial period is somewhat like going away to college and coming back in the summer to live with our parents; we can never quite fully believe in our parent's worldview anymore because we have tasted a completely new one. Even though the power of ego and the inertia of karma can be quite incredible, and some folks will come back to their ego and again make a home in their minds; there will always be this little voice of intuition that knows that ego is not the complete truth. The power of awakening and evolution is quite incredible and so is the power of habit and ego; it is up to the individual and what they value *to determine* where they will ultimately make their home.

Some of us may wonder why some teachers, who claim to be enlightened, do not fully embody their teachings or still trip over their egoic conditioning: this is because the power of egoic conditioning is strong, and they happen to be humans *just like us* living in a never ending evolving world. If we have any question about our life and our growth we can look to our life as a mirror. Life is always presenting us with our next step, in growth. If we look in the mirror of our life, we can see who we are in our expression of Divinity and where we need to grow. What we find is that the saner our life is, the closer we are to our liberation or enlightenment, because Life has worked through our major life lessons within us, within our lives. Nirvana is often said to be the burning out of the flames of our mind; in a sense, liberation or nirvana is the quietness of our mind and its mirrored reflection in our life and our being. For the majority of us who still struggle with ourselves, we can be happy because we have the opportunity to see where we need to grow in the mirror of our life. Where we are struggling with life and others is our evolving edge. This experience simply points us in the direction of where we still have more work to do. It is important to remember that as long as we are in human form, we will be growing in some way or another; this is the purpose of this world. If we see this as a problem and resist what Life is showing us, then we will suffer. If we see our arising drama and conditioning with humility and an openness, it will be much easier to let go of whatever we continue to trip over.

It is wise, not to get too enamored with ourselves when we first wake up, especially in the transcendent period, because eventually, we come back down into our body and egoic consciousness again, and humbly laugh. We laugh because in our humanity, we realize how much work there is to do. However because we have a new orientation, a vast perspective, and our relationship with suffering has tremendously changed, in a paradoxical way, even while we struggle with difficulty, we struggle less, because we are no longer resisting what's in front of us. We continue letting go and surrendering until, we no longer are resisting the Divinity that we are. This process does not have to take lifetimes; it can begin right here and right now, just as we are. As we sincerely show up to the very process of awakening, we have this wonderful opportunity to consciously give ourselves to this movement until this Movement becomes Us.

What follows are a collection of reflections, teachings, writings, and personal experiences written over the period of many years that weave together what this radical shift called *Awakening* is. Even though Awakening is quite an impersonal shift, (impersonal in the sense that it is beyond ego or a personal sense of self) I wanted to share a perspective from my humanity. Many books are written from monasteries or ashrams, or by individuals who seem to have life completely worked out in some perfected spiritual sense. But for me this is not the case, life is ever unfolding, ever changing and the divine expression of our humanity is never *fully* worked out—our lives are never fully worked out, because we are *ever evolving*. I write with humility, from this ever unfolding place, where our lives are messy, growing, transforming, yet ever evolving forward. I know some teachers do not like to admit their humanity or speak in any way about themselves. Yet in order for me to be honest about this expression of divinity, I must absolutely include my individual humanity in my teaching. We are individuals, and often there is a bias against being human in the spiritual world, because the human world is messy and where we get into so much trouble. But there is nothing wrong with being human; it is actually a tremendous gift, our lives are where the Divine becomes incarnate in form, in matter. The fact that we are amazingly alive shows we are Divine. What else could animate our body and minds if it were not the Divine? How could being human ever be a problem? It is only our minds that have a problem with who we are.

Yet, if we want to be fully free, we must be willing to love all of life, even our very own egoic nature, which paradoxically is the Divine as well. No aspect of Life is outside of Divinity. Many books are written from a perspective of impersonal Enlightenment. I wanted to share both the impersonal and personal, because that is what it is like to be human, whether we are a Buddha or someone full of egoic personality, we all have a personal individual nature. I feel it is important to include both our humanity and our Divinity; we have denied one or the other for ages, but both are God. I share in an effort to create a deep understanding of what it is like to be human and awake. If my experience comes off as being grandiose, forgive me. In my humanity I know myself to be quite ordinary, yet in our Divinity we are beyond incredible. There is a value in seeing how spiritual awakening and being human meet in an ordinary Life in relationship with our partners, our kids, families and friends, with our busy lives, in divorce, illness, death, careers and all of life. This book is a call to awakening and embracing and transforming our humanity. Some share the beauty of music or art, and in this book I share myself, my humanity and Beauty. But this Beauty does not only belong to me, this Beauty is your Beauty and God's Beauty. All of us are made of the same wonder, from this place I offer myself.

Questioning our self created Reality

Our minds provide us with an artificial sense of security from assuming we know how life works, what's true and what's not true, who is good, who is bad and so on. We received this knowing from our past environments, from our parents, our schools, and our culture. Almost every thought we have has been given to us. But if we are honest we really have no idea how life works, how any of it works, beyond what we have been told; we have no idea if what we *think* is actually true. If we are honest we see that life is a giant mystery. Our very thoughts and thinking mind arise out of the essence of this mystery. Every aspect of this life arises out of this mystery. If we want to be free, we will give ourselves to this mystery. If we want to live in the land of egoic knowing, we will simply believe our habitual and conditioned thoughts and never question this arising mind within us. But if we want to unknow the reality of our egos, we will begin to question them—we will question everything we think and feel on every level.

If we take the time to deeply investigate this, what we find is that we know very little about the nature of our mind and thoughts and yet, we base our entire lives on what arises in our minds. If we take a few minutes to examine and question this mysterious movement which arises within us, we will find a greater mystery than we ever imagined. To reflect in this way we have to be willing to stop, and literally step out of our mind so that we can gain a perspective of this mysterious dance of mind. As we do, we find that a seemingly random display of thoughts floats into our consciousness throughout our waking and dreaming hours in a wondrous and completely mysterious way. Shockingly, none of us actually know what thoughts *are*, or ever take the time to question them, yet many of us are willing to fight for these mostly unconscious and conditioned movements of mind. Because we do not stop and examine this dance of mind, we unconsciously mistake these impersonal thoughts to be ours and base our entire life on them. But if we do stop and look—what we find is that we really have no idea what thoughts *actually are*, where they come from, or whether they are true or not. This can be a shocking realization, because our human reality is almost completely based on what we think.

Spiritual awakening begins with the investigation of this dance. Our whole self-created reality begins to crumble, with a few basic questions, such as: Am I sure that I want what my mind tells me I want? Do I know that what I think is actually true? Can I choose to believe or not believe my very own thoughts? If so, what does this mean about my perception of reality and the character of *me* that I have built upon these perceptions? Who am I beyond these impersonal thoughts? Where do my thoughts arise from? As we step in the direction of questioning, we begin to step into the mysterious presence that we are which is beyond our egoic thinking mind.

From this place beyond thought, we can deeply investigate this core illusion of mind. One of the greatest illusions that humanity suffers from is the belief that our thoughts actually *mean* something. To deeply examine this we have to be willing to take some time and sit with the question: *do thoughts have inherent meaning?* This means we may sit with this question and deeply contemplate it for an hour, a day or a lifetime. Upon deeper reflection on whether or not thoughts possess an inherent meaning, what we find is that our thoughts' meaning is automatically and unconsciously determined by *us*, based on our past conditioning, education and experience of life; essentially this is an unconscious process biased by what we have been taught about life. Very few individuals are actually awake enough to consciously decide what our very thoughts mean. When we are awake, we see that our thoughts actually do not have any inherent truth or meaning to them and remain meaningless until, we assign them a meaning. Unfortunately for most of the population, 95% of the time, this dance happens unconsciously. Almost always, this meaning that we give our thoughts is automatically given through our lens of projection—the lens of our past experience of life.

Yet, if we are consciously present with what arises in our minds, we can *choose* which meaning to assign to the thoughts that arise within us and radically recreate our experience of life. Yet if we are living in an unconscious way then our ego will habitually and automatically assign meaning to the thoughts that drift through our minds. It assigns this meaning based on our perception of our past experiences of life, which is based on our upbringing, our hopes and fears, our culture and collective consciousness. We all have had the experience of being with an old friend and then someone new walks in the room. In this situation, we have no idea who this new person is and yet we may have one experience of this person and our old friend may have a radically different experience of the same person. Perhaps we really like the new person and our old friend, who had the exact same encounter as us, does not like them.

The reason this happens is because we all see life through a projection of our past and then based on that information, we assign meaning to our experience of the present. So it is not necessarily *the experience* that determines what we think of it, it is our projection that determines what we experience, which we then unconsciously interpret to be the truth of the situation. When we unconsciously assign meaning to everything we think, we create a story; this unconsciously created story, now becomes our version of reality. Take for example the statement, "I got a speeding ticket." This is just a simple statement. If we simply allow this statement to be, there is no problem. But not many people can just allow this statement to be without commenting on it or adding meaning to it. Our minds automatically come forward in a flash of a second, and assign meaning to this statement. Our minds may judge that this is bad or that we deserved this, or didn't deserve this, based on our projection of the fairness of life. The story that our minds adds to this experience distorts reality. The simple reality is that we received a speeding ticket, yet notice how our reality changes when we assign the meaning: *and this is unfair, I did not deserve this, other people were going faster*. We can see how quickly our ego can determine whether or not something is good or bad.

When we believe in this story and decide that our story is "true," we create a division between us and the direct experience of Reality and suffer in the realm of duality or the world of right and wrong, good and bad. If we want to be free, we are invited to instead see life from a nonperspective or from the equanimity that comes from simply allowing life to be as it is. Imagine if we get a speeding ticket and then simply pay the ticket without any commenting on what happened. If we can simply allow life to be as it is, (which is all that is really required) we step into the inherent freedom of all of life. Yet, if we engage and indulge in our story of how life should be, we can spend a long time suffering.

Our constant invitation is to simply allow life to be as it is and take care of what arises in a practical way. I can remember that I once was married and then some time later, divorced. My former partner at some point moved on and started dating; this was the objective truth. Yet when my ego experienced this, it had so many comments, beliefs and judgments and created a huge story of why this was somehow *wrong* for our kids. Our friends and families also had their own array of comments and judgments; this is the nature of the mind—to judge and comment on life. Yet the more I thought about what was happening and indulged in my judgments, the more I suffered. But ultimately, I stopped suffering, when I was able to see this new experience without commenting on it or judging it in my mind. For this to happen, I had to let go of my allegiance with and indulgence in my very own thoughts and trust that Life was more intelligent than me. I had to accept that life was in control, not me. As I stopped commenting on this experience and let go more and more into the direct experience of this moment—and finally, fully accepted this new experience, I became free of it. I was able to look at this new person and see him for who he was—an embodiment of the Divine. As I let go and embraced what was present in my new reality, I smiled again and fell on my knees as my heart broke open and began to see the Beauty of Life everywhere.

To live in this open hearted way, we must be willing to stop believing that our thoughts *mean* something. We need to stop believing that our thoughts are true. We don't need to stop thinking; that may never happen. Even if we have incredible discipline and self control, we may never stop our minds or fully control our thoughts. But what we can do is stop *believing* in them; we can stop believing in the meaning that is habitually and mechanically assigned to our random thoughts. If one watches the *thinking* that arises within, we see that a random stream of thoughts just come and go, and some of these thoughts our minds determine are important and then assigns a great deal of meaning to and as a result, we become attached to our desires, agendas, ideas, and we suffer. But if we realize that our thoughts have no inherent meaning, that they are meaningless or empty, we can be free of the suffering that comes when we attach to them. As we step into this great freedom which is here all the time, we discover that we no longer need to fight for or against anything because of our habitual egoic tendencies. We can give up the struggle with what is. As we let go in this way, we experience the relief of constantly struggling with life. As a result, we can then truly choose to use our energy for what is important. We can see what is happening in a clear way and respond from a place of peace and empowerment, instead of responding from a place of habitual and conditioned meaningless resistance to what is.

The Buddha once said, "I gained nothing from supreme Enlightenment and for that very reason it is called supreme enlightenment." Most think that with Enlightenment we gain some never ending good feeling, but this is not what he is telling us; what he is transmitting to us is that Enlightenment is not a game of gaining, it is a process of subtraction. If we give up all the commenting on and about our experience which is really adding extra meaning and judgment to everything we think—if we can give up this dance, we will be free. We will be free when we see life for what it is, without the commentary. Life really opens when we live in this hugeness that is beyond our commenting minds. As we stop indulging in this dance of mentality, so much energy is freed up and we relax in this nonperspective where we no longer live in opposition to life and begin to live as Life Itself.

Being Willing

If we want to change, grow and awaken, we have to be willing to meet our pain and every aspect of ourselves that we avoid with a total unconditional loving presence. To do this, we must first be willing to see all the difficult parts of ourselves with honesty. Not only do we need to be able to see them, but we also need to be willing to be fully open to them. We need to be open with all of ourselves, which includes being willing to *feel* these difficult parts. Most people are somewhat ok with *seeing* a difficult emotion or painful aspect of themselves, but when asked to actually *feel* and experience that emotion, they turn away and find anything else to do. But if we want an emotion or some deep pattern within us to change or transform, we have to be willing to give it our full attention. To be free means that we do not hide from anything—especially the difficult and painful parts of ourselves. To be free in this way, we have to be fully willing to meet them with our own love and compassion and acceptance so that we can attend to what's here and not turn away. We practically, do this through being willing to *feel* what's here even if it is uncomfortable. When we fully feel an emotion in this way it naturally begins to heal and release. But if we continue to ignore it, the pain will simply simmer below the surface, until one day when we can no longer repress it, and we are forced to feel it and acknowledge what is still within us and attend to our healing work. We can choose to do this work consciously through meeting what arises in each moment or unconsciously deny what's here, while living in fear of that which is uncomfortable.

Being free does not only mean that we are able to be open and honest with all the difficult parts of ourselves. It also means that we are willing to see our own Beauty and Spaciousness as well. And a funny thing happens when most people look at their own Beauty and Spaciousness; they become scared—scared because they never knew this to be themselves. Or scared because they know this is the Truth of themselves, and if they are going to live from that place they must give up all the silliness of their own minds (all their thoughts and opinions about themselves and others). Or perhaps, scared because of knowing themselves as something totally new is so foreign to them and they would have to give up their old identities. Most people are really scared of something new—especially being something new and unknown; which means we may have to be willing to be uncomfortable for some time as we adjust to being a greater and more expanded version of ourselves. The biggest fear that most seekers face is that in embodying this Beauty, they will somehow die. It is true in a sense that there will be a death. It is a death of the ego as the forefront of our consciousness. The ego will certainly still be there, but it will take the back seat to this Beauty and Spacious Consciousness that we are. Our constant invitation is for us to be willing to walk into the unknown, and embrace whatever arises, as we discover once again our own Radiant Self.

Spiritual vs. Egoic Freedom.

When most of us think of freedom we think of being able to do whatever we want to do. This is the kind of freedom that our ego wants. If we live unconsciously our ego will continue this dance of trying to do whatever it wants, whenever it wants to. But spiritual freedom is vastly different. Spiritual freedom is about giving up ego (our wants, desires, opinions, beliefs, agendas and attachments), and being in total alignment with who and what we are, *which in our deepest sense*, means being in alignment with the will of the Divine. Spiritual freedom ironically, is the giving up of all our egoic wants, desires and agendas. Our ego actually gets nothing out of the pursuit of liberation, except its own disillusionment; and when we allow ourselves to be disillusioned, we begin to see clearly for the first time. We begin to see the true nature of Reality, and we wake up and see that we are one *with* all of Life and the very movement of Life. We experience a beautiful *oneness* when we stop believing in the dividing nature of ego, because when we allow the walls of ego to drop. Or put a different way, when we stop believing our thoughts or feelings as the truth of life and simply begin to directly experience life outside the lens of egoic division—we discover that we are one with all of life; we discover that who and what we are is in no way separate from *anything*.

To allow for the great disillusionment of our self created reality of our minds, we must be willing to let go of everything we hold onto and believe in. We must be willing to let go of our cherished ideas and opinions, our likes and dislikes, and more importantly, our self image. Most of us though, are unwilling to give up all of this. For most of us, our thoughts and ideas and self image are what we think we are. But this is not the truth of what we are. When we hold on to these things, what we get in return is a limited *self* created by our mind and a limited experience. This is what our mind does; it creates itself again and again through building a world—a self, an image—out of thoughts and ideas.

When we believe in this image, we suffer. We suffer because we go from being big, open spaciousness to being a mask in some form or another, a limited self image. We go from silent and free awareness to "Look at me. Look how successful I am. I am a Doctor" or "a nondual teacher," and yet when we still feel empty inside of our mask of identity, we continue to suffer.

As long as we identify with our self-created image, we will experience pain. But if we are willing to live and be more than our mask, we can be free. We become free when we identify with the hugeness of Reality instead of the masks of our mind. When we identify with our sky-like nature, it is much more difficult to become attached to being *this* person who is having a problem or with *this* person who is wanting *this* or *that* to be happy. The sky is open to everything and does not complain or try to hold onto if *this* comes or *that* goes. Our mind, on the other hand is wired to see a black or white dualistic way of perceiving. As we step into our true nature, we step into an all embracing unity. As we step into our minds, we step into divisiveness and, as a result, we suffer. In a sense, the more we relate to life from a personal perspective (*my personal wants and desires*), the more *meness* we have or the more self we have, the more we suffer; because there is more self present to argue with what is. We have all seen individuals with big egos—they tend to suffer more. The opposite is true also; the less ego or self or *meness* we have, the less we suffer. The less self we have, the *vaster* we become. It is actually that we are already vast, yet our vast or sky-like nature is eclipsed by our egoic self image. The good news is that we are already this vastness and as we let go of ego, our hugeness is what is already here, and has always been here. Our freedom comes from stepping out of our self created identity of mind and into who and what we are: limitless vastness beyond expression.

Surrender Changes Everything

In the ancient Zen tradition, there is a story about a peasant with an ox on a string. He has a big ox (his ego) and he leads it around with a little string. The string may represent mindfulness or right effort. But in the beginning, when we first step on the path, we need a heavy duty rope to control our egos and so, we must practice diligently and exert our will power until we can tame our mind and emotions. Eventually, after we have trained ourselves through discipline, if we want to continue on the path, we must give up the very control that we have gained through our practices. And we are invited to fully surrender any and all sense of perceived egoic control or resistance to what is. We learn to give up the fight, to give up resisting, controlling and manipulating life, and then we no longer need a thick rope to keep our egos in line; we just need a simple string to keep ourselves in alignment with Reality. To surrender this deeply we must be willing to fall on our knees and give everything to life and be open to receiving everything from life, until we see no difference between who and what we think we are and Life Itself. This process of surrender, of letting go may take a day, a month or years depending on how stubborn and controlling we are. But it is possible for all of us to let go completely if we are sincere, innocent and willing.

There are so many times in life when we have fought against things we have no control over. By fighting against life, we unconsciously and arrogantly assume we know better than life or assume we can control Life. I can remember a number of years ago, when I was a young dad working three different jobs and going to school. I was pulled in about eight different directions. The amount of tension in my body was overwhelming; at any moment I was ready to explode. Needless to say, I could not keep it all together and I became so angry with God. I began to hate God for creating suffering in the world. When I look back at it all, I have to laugh at how confused my perspective was. God didn't create suffering just to make us suffer. I was suffering, because I did not know how to let go. I was suffering because I was trying to hold on to too much. I was literally trying to hold things together that didn't want to be together. I was trying to do too many things at once and was unwilling to let any of them go, thinking that I was so necessary and important *that life needed me* to micromanage every aspect of my life. It was pure arrogance; life didn't need my hands in everything for life to happen, yet how many of us suffer from this same delusion?

We experience suffering when we resist what is; when we resist the movement of life. I was resisting life by trying to do everything myself and not allowing life to unfold. Day after day I was fighting and not going to win at any of it. Our egos don't like to let go or to be defeated and so I kept fighting. When we resist, we become like the angry ox pulling the peasant around the pasture in the old Zen stories. As long as we fight with life, we will suffer. But the sooner the ox surrenders, the easier life will become. When we are the ox, we have to learn to give up, and when we give up fully—we become free to enjoy life as it is; we settle down and become happy. This surrender comes from giving ourselves permission to radically slow down, to relax, to breathe, to open our eyes and see the big open sky and green pastures. To be free, to be happy, we have to be willing to become empty of *this want* and *that want*, of *this idea* and *that idea*. When we give up our agendas, our desire for control, our attachments, we relax and let go and we become free, we become content. But we will never be free if we are constantly being pulled this way or that way, by our mind and fighting with it all.

Many mistakenly believe that we are our mind. But, this is not the case. The mind is a conditioned movement of psychological forces that have nothing to do with us. It may come as a shock to some, to hear that we are not the movement of these forces. These forces simply arise within us without our permission and without us asking for them. These forces were given to us by our biology, our culture, and our parents. Without these forces, we still very much exist. We are that which exists beyond the movements of mind; prior to these forces we existed and

49

once these forces leave us, we will still be here. We are that which exists always, before, during and after the movements of mind. We can see the truth of this right now. If we sit quietly and simply *see*— thoughts, beliefs and memories simply arise and fall away in our consciousness. They come and go on their own. When we were born and our mind was empty, we existed. When our minds become silent, we exist. And when our mind gets worked up by desire or attachment, we can notice this desire or attachment within ourselves. We must be that which is beyond thought, because we can observe thought. If we were our thoughts, we would be as fleeting as our thoughts, coming and going in and out of existence so quickly. But we are not our minds; we are that which can see the movement of mind, that which is Aware. And this Awareness that we are has no beginning or end, no boundary.

There is a cautionary note that goes with the teachings of letting go of control and accepting what is. This is in no way an invitation to be a doormat. If action is required, we act in alignment with the highest wisdom, with the highest good. To do this we must ask our hearts, and listen for the guidance from the quiet voice of our heart. If we ask our mind it will give us a long argument. If we ask our emotions, they will offer us an emotional reaction. But when we listen to our heart, it will come like the clear sound of a bell. And from this place we may be called to act. If we are in danger or being abused, by all means, we do what is necessary to protect ourselves. Sometimes people misinterpret the teachings on letting go and they give up all effort or doing; this is not the kind of surrender I am speaking about. Sometimes surrender means doing a very difficult job, or standing up to someone who is abusive, or having the courage to leave a relationship from a place of strength and love. In this way, letting go and right action become the same movement, because they originate from the same place—from listening to the movement of the Divine in us, as Us. To listen this deeply, we have slow down and breathe, because when there are five or six different voices within all fighting for our attention, it is difficult to hear the quiet soft voice of the Divine. To do this, we may need to forgive or forget, or let go, or stand up, or heal. This is Life's challenge for us to come into a complete unity with It. To be this unified, we must do whatever is necessary to bring our big ox into a gentle, yet total surrender.

Steps to Clarity

To see clearly, it is absolutely necessarily that we must first separate who we *are* from what we think. Most of us believe that we are what we think, but we are not our thoughts. To discover this, we must learn to step into the one who is aware, the one who simply sees, the one who is reading this page. To continue living lost in the dream of mind, we simply have to follow the inertia of our mind's movement taking us where ever it leads, unconsciously believing in and being seduced by its dance. If we look honestly at our experience all day and night, we go in and out of dreams: dreams of the past, dreams of the future, dreams of romance and dreams of disaster, all the time our mind is busy dreaming, while the beauty of the present moment goes by unnoticed.

To see clearly, it is helpful to take some time *to stop* whatever we are doing. It is extremely helpful in this inquiry, for us to first slow down our breath and to become aware of ourselves in every level and aspect of our being. That means we become mindful of our body, the sensations within ourselves, our emotions, and our *spiritual energetic nature* or the feeling of the energy that animates our being. Once we have slowed down and become deeply aware of ourselves, we can begin the process of separating who we are from what we think. It is important to not rush any aspect of this, if we want to truly step out of our mind's dream.

What follows are the basic steps to this process: Take the time to fully stop and stay with the practice until the end. Do not believe anything you think. Open your eyes and look around and see that there is no real immediate problem right here in this moment. *There is no problem right here;* this means we do not believe anything our mind is telling us about having a problem. Our mind always is handing us things to worry about, or to criticize, or to do—but we do not have to engage in this dance in any way. If we join in this dance, we will again find ourselves unconsciously dreaming. Of course, if we do see real physical danger, we immediately take care of it. If we are standing in front of a moving bus, we get out of the way. Other than a real immediate physical danger, the instructions here are to not believe what you think while we do this practice.

Notice that beyond our thoughts, there is one who is just seeing life unfold. Bring your full attention to the one who is just seeing. Take some time and just *see*. Allow yourself to be fully identified with just seeing. Focus on one object in your environment for a minute and let go of any thoughts that come and simply be with what you are seeing. If the thoughts continue to arise—do not believe them or get involved with them for some time. Just *see* right here, right now. Stare at a wall, the sky, a mirror and allow your attention to remain in one place without moving.

Notice that when we focus on something without commenting on it or believing the comments that our minds make, we directly experience a tangible oneness with whatever is in front of us. Take another minute and just *see*, and directly experience *seeing*. Notice how when we just see, we feel expanded, as if we have no boundaries—like there are no walls between us and all of life, and in this boundaryless perspective we see that there is a perfect alive innocence to all life.

Notice that this *seeing* does not have a problem, judgment, need to act or agenda, we are just *seeing*. To stay clear, we resist the temptation to believe our thoughts and judgments, and arguments about life, and we simply see and act from this quiet innocence that we are. If we want to suffer, we simply have to believe the arguments that arise in the mind and allow ourselves to be lost in the dream of the past and future and miss the alive, innocent, ineffable oneness of this moment. If we want to be free, we give ourselves to this innocence and allow this innocence to move us in every aspect of our lives. At some point we will laugh when we realize that we no longer have to do a practice to stay awake, that we are awake and actually have been this whole time, gently watching the dream go by.

The quick version:
Slow down to a stop;
Don't believe your thoughts;
Just see. Notice or directly experience the seeing;
Don't believe your thoughts;
Allow yourself to be the ineffable innocence that we are when we just see.

Beyond Defending We Become Everything

When I first began to study spirituality many years ago, I quickly understood that the "ego" was the primary obstacle between us and freedom. I can remember hearing countless teachings about how one had to get rid of this thing called "ego" or go through some process of "ego death" in order to be free. Yet no one clearly explained what the ego actually was. Ignorantly and with great enthusiasm, for many years I tried very hard to get rid of my ego with my spiritual practices, but was rarely successful in the least bit. I was so unsuccessful with achieving *ego death* and confused by this mysterious thing called *ego* that I began to study psychology and quickly became even more confused. I noticed that psychologist and spiritual teachers alike, use many different and often conflicting definitions for the ego. While in graduate school, I saw that almost every theorist created their own definition of the term ego which made discussions among schools of psychology very confusing. Everyone from psychologists, to counselors, to psychiatrists to spiritual teachers were using the term *ego* quite differently and as a result, the teachings were not clear (the same confusion happens with the word "awakening"). I found that many of the uses of the word "ego" by psychologists were quite healthy and necessary for our functioning and survival in the world, and many of the spiritual definitions were referring to pride, judgmentalism, arrogance, self centeredness, attachment and desire. As a result of this confusion, many spiritual folks were trying to get rid of healthy aspects of functioning in the pursuit of ego death. And many individuals who first studied psychology and later turned to spirituality did not understand why the ego needed to be removed from oneself. After many years of personally struggling with this confusion, I formed my own definition of ego and decided to no longer go to war with my ego. Instead, I decided to attempt to truly understand my egoic mind first in a friendly way, before I tried to get rid of it. Later, I discovered the very act or attempt to try to get rid of ego is actually an egoic desire and in truth not actually even up to us anyway. One of the great gifts my Teacher gave me was continually reminding us to examine our egos with an attitude of universal friendliness. Having this attitude changed everything and lead to incredible openings; whereas, anytime I tried to get rid of anything within myself tended to lead to more of the very thing I thought I needed to rid of.

Because the word *ego* has been defined and is used in so many different ways, it is important to first clarify what I am speaking about when I use the term ego. For the purposes of this book, I will offer a very basic definition. The ego is simply *a collection of psychological forces arising to orient ourselves toward a safe existence in this world*. These forces arise so that we are seamlessly oriented toward life and continue to exist in a way which seeks pleasure and avoids pain. This basically means that we *know* who and what we are and have a consistent identity which continues to exist in a way with more pleasure and the avoidance of pain. For example, we may have the egoic identity of being a mother, and our ego will support this identity by continually reminding us who we are with the arising of mothering thoughts—this way we will continue to have a consistent identity. Our ego would not be doing its job if we had thoughts in one moment of being a mother, and in the next of being a race car driver, and then of being a child, and then of being a tree. If our ego did not operate properly, we would not have a solid identity and we would not be able to operate in the world in a sane way. The job of a healthy ego is to provide us with a consistent identity from which we can operate in the world. In addition to providing us an identity, our ego protects our identity and our body from harm. In no way is an ego good or bad it is simply a psychological force or state of consciousness that allows *what we are* (a vast luminous cognizant spiritual being) to operate in the world. From a metaphysical perspective, we are all formless and fearless souls who live as the vast space of absolute divinity, yet who incarnate and take on the role of a character so that Life has the opportunity to evolve. When we take on the role of a character, we are also taking on the psychological forces of ego, which is essentially a defense mechanism and pleasure seeking mechanism. This defense mechanism attempts to protect our character from being harmed, and attempts to experience the most amount of pleasure. However, these forces are more like a mask or a coat of armor, than a true identity. They are simply forces with no inherent *solid* egoic self behind them. Yet if we believe or take the empty masks to be ourselves, we will always feel empty and seek to fill it with something "solid." But we will never be successful in this, because everything in this world is impermanent, and what we are is spacious emptiness, that goes on forever, making it impossible to be able to ever fill this void. It does not matter how many objects we acquire or relationships we have, nothing will fill this void—this spacious aware emptiness that is our true undivided nature.

Most individuals are afraid of this void within, not many know that we *are* this spacious emptiness. And because we are afraid of not knowing what we are or discovering ourselves as emptiness, we align with our egoic identity and as long as we choose to align with our egoic identity, we will be subject to the rules and forces of ego. Because most of humanity is lost in this dance of ego, of seeking pleasure and avoiding pain, they continue seeking in the realm of ego. The way out of this dance is to investigate these psychological forces and discover their illusion. When we see through the illusion, what we discover is what remains beyond this illusion—our timeless, fearless, existence as All that Is. To realize this, we must first, (in an open hearted way) inquire into what the ego is, so that we can live in a way that is beyond it.

Like an onion, when we peel through the layers, we simply find more layers, but no essential core; this is true also of our ego. When we get to the last layer and peel it away there *is no thing* there that is solid, tangible, or fixed; there is no essential core identity found in our egoic nature. This can be quite shocking, if we really examine it. This identification with the layers of ego, with our hopes and fears, desires and attachments, pleasures and aversions as who and what we are, is the great illusion. We hope and believe that we are *something*, that there is something to be found in the depths of our ego, because when we attach ourselves to an identity, a mask, our ego relaxes and experiences a brief sense of being settled. But because this egoic identity is not the truth of us, intuitively we keep searching and do not rest. We all can remember being in adolescence and not knowing who we were and then had the experience of latching onto some form of identity, such as being a jock or a geek or a punk and feeling a part of a group and experiencing a temporary feeling of acceptance. This illusion of completion through finding an identity continues throughout our lives. Perhaps later on in life, we create a spiritual identity as a yogi or a Buddhist, but this too is just as false as the rest of the masks that we wear and deep within, we know it, which is why we continue to seek.

Ironically at the ego's core is not some solid self, but spacious, luminous emptiness and surrounding this essence are our impersonal primal layers of ego. These layers of impersonal psychological defenses serve to protect us from harm and have been essential for our survival. Also here are our fundamental beliefs about ourselves, which usually consist of our beliefs regarding our inherent unworthiness. These beliefs that we are somehow unworthy, lacking or deficient, fuel our search for completion. After years of investigation, inquiry, therapy, and spiritual practice, I have yet to find some inherent solid egoic core self. There are layers and layers of ego, yet after all the layers are seen through, what we find is not some "egoic me" who is lacking and needs to be healed, but our inherent Divinity. This realization can be so hilarious for us as we discover, that all this time when we identified with our egoic self, our story or personal drama, we really thought we were some *thing* important or something that needed to be defended or something unworthy, yet none of it is actually true; there is no solid or fixed egoic sense of self that needs anything or could be given anything to become somehow complete. If there is a solid or fixed thing called ego, we would be able to point to it, but we can't. When we close our eyes and look for it, what we find is nothing, simply *blank, open space*. We can even close our eyes right now and look inside; do we tangibly find anything besides luminous space? If we really look for our ego, which we are always fighting with and trying to get rid of, and defending where is this ego? Is the belief, *I am a yogi,* really who we are? If we changed our spiritual orientation would we still exist? Of course we would. Our mind, our thoughts, beliefs and memories are not who we are. Yet we treat them like they are real, like they are another person in the room. We talk to it, analyze it, fight with it, but in reality our ego cannot even be found. Ironically we have spent years painfully defending this *thing* that does not exist beyond a movement of imagination in our minds. It would be much more accurate to say, *my ego is a product of my imagination*, than *who I am*.

As I investigated into this I was amazed to find that what I *am* is separate from my imagination; that my imagination arises within me, that what I am is the witness to this arising movement of psychological forces. When I look deeply, what I discover is that this ego is a movement of arising impersonal psychological forces—a movement of images or phenomena with nothing *real* behind them. The Buddha told us a long time ago, that the egoic self is an illusion. Not many of us like to hear this, because most of us think of ourselves or imagine ourselves as something important or something unworthy. When we sincerely look and directly find a vast empty space within, with movements of imaginations within this space—it can be shattering to our sense of self and this shattering is the beginning of our liberation. As we directly look, we may not find anything permanent and solid like we have imagined or assumed ourselves to be, yet what we do find is a very wonderful essential essence. This essence is empty of egoic identity, yet spacious, luminous and aware.

I can remember one day being in the heat of a difficult argument with my partner because I was not honest about something I had done at work. I was withholding what had happen, because I thought that if she knew what happened, she might become upset. As we argued, I felt blamed for acting in foolish and unconscious ways and began to get angry at her. Throughout my life, I can admit that often I have acted like a fool and then proceeded to defend my foolishness. Yet, this time as I began to argue and defend why I was not wrong, something startling happened—I saw that maybe perhaps, I didn't need to defend myself. In a fraction of a second my whole egoic defense system temporarily disappeared; and with this disappearance came a realization that *what I was defending* did not did not matter and the very act of defending *it* only lead to more suffering. Furthermore, what I saw was that the *I* that I thought I needed to defend did not exist. By this I mean all the thoughts of *me,* this person, who had *these* beliefs, opinions, stories about myself and my life, and all the egoic defensiveness necessary to maintain this identity had spontaneously fallen away. As I stood there with a blank look in my eyes and the experience of complete emptiness, my partner became confused, because I had nothing to say and was no longer arguing. I had been pulled into the present moment and stood naked with nothing to defend. I became quite disoriented in this new reality, because for so long I had felt like I needed to defend myself or else something painful would happen. But as I looked under the veil of the defensive mechanical thought pattern that *I needed to defend myself*, what I found was empty space and the experience of total unity. And this space and unity did not need to be defended against anyone's actions or words. I realized that I was the one, who had witnessed this whole dance of being foolish, being in an argument and thinking I needed to defend myself from my partner. I saw that I did not have to defend myself against Life, and especially with the one who I was in close relationship with. After all, how could I be hurt by my very own Self? This discovery, made it quite easy for me to listen, apologize and show up as love, which is really what we all want in life. Over the years, I have found that it is much easier to be love—to be ourselves, if all of our energy is not busy defending an imaginary egoic existence.

I can imagine that this shift in my consciousness out of ego and into love came from a willingness to question the ego at every turn. If my ego came forward and said, *this person should not be doing this*, I may ask myself, "Is it true that they should not be doing this? Do I know better than Life, what should and should not be?" I would laugh, because this *is what's happening* and as long as I argue with reality, I suffer. Often while investigating my reactions toward life, I would notice that there are certain behaviors people can do that make my egoic defenses arise. As each defense would arise, I would question it. I would ask, "Is this defense necessary? Who am I trying to protect?" When I looked, all I found were sensations of insecurity arising within the space of my presence. Next, I would ask, "what would happen if I did not defend this space, would I be ok?" And I found that, often fear would arise out of my belly, yet as I met this fear with an absolute love, by taking the time to breath into it and hold a space to honor it, it quickly passed and I was very much ok. But if I made the mistake of trying to defend my ego, I would consistently suffer, and then find myself lost again defending my imagined self. But if I let myself be undefended, I would experience feelings and sensations arising within a space of freedom; some of these feelings and sensations felt uncomfortable, some painful and anxious, but ultimately they were seen and felt simply as sensations arising in the space of my awareness. On a practical level, when we can experience all reactions as simply energy moving through us, we become free. This freedom becomes available when we are willing to stop and fully feel what is arising within us, without getting involved in any way with the story or thoughts that are linked to the sensations. Any time we find ourselves experiencing conflict, we can allow our body to remind us to simply feel what is here fully and lovingly, and to let it all pass by in the vastness that we are. As we do this work, we become free and unified with all of Life, because we are no longer maintaining walls against life.

Awakening is an invitation for us to strip away our unconscious self-created importance, our layers of personality and defensive psychological forces, and then to begin to know what we truly are beyond our egoic personality. As we do this, we become free of ego, free of self and paradoxically free to be the beauty of our essential nature. As the layers of ego fall away what we are left with is our innate Divinity, which is perfect and clear. But to begin to know this Divinity as ourselves, we must first let go of, or see through that which we are not. As we begin to see clearly from the perspective of our innate Divinity, we begin to realize that the more self or personality we have, the more we will suffer, and the less self we have, the freer we are. We all know the experience of having lots of ideas, attachments, agendas, opinions, and expectations—the more of this we have, the more we will suffer. Yet, if we have very little of this, then there is not much material for us to trip over or become confused by or attached to. To fully understand this it is important to know what these layers of ego are and how they fool us into thinking we have a solid, fixed and important self, which will then be experienced as a *me* who will perceive itself as separate from the rest of life. This belief in separation is what ultimately causes our suffering.

When the Buddha said there is no solid or permanent self, he did not mean there was absolutely nothing there. He meant that we are not solid and fixed like our ego presents us to be. If we assume that we are fixed and solid, then we also may assume that there is something within us that needs to be defended. But what exactly are we defending? If the ego is simply a fabrication of mental thoughts, images, and conditioning, why do we need to defend this? What are we really upholding, besides a movement of impersonal psychological forces? Yet, of course, if there is real danger, it is wise to listen to our egoic defense mechanisms. But because many of us, no longer live in physically dangerous environments the majority of the time, it isn't necessary to listen to or act out all of our egoic defenses that arise for example, when someone challenges our point of view or cuts us off in traffic. Yet when we choose to rest in our essential nature, a wonderful intelligence arises that can guide us to act in an intelligent and skillful way, which may be quite different than our habitual defenses and reactions toward life.

This movement of ego, which is essentially a play of fabricated psychological forces, is the very thing that we go to war for: our ideas, our beliefs, and our opinions. Many of us right now on this planet are fighting with each other, because of a deeply held belief or dogma, or even because we are scared to open and trust in the goodness of life and each other. We hold onto our egoic defenses and meet life from fear and separation, instead of love and unity. It takes a tremendous courage and humility to live beyond our tightly held beliefs, opinions and egoic defenses. If we are willing, we can begin to see that these places where we identify cause a painful separation between us and Life; and then we can begin to see that there is another way to live that is beyond what our very minds are telling us about life.

Before we step into this greater Reality, it can be helpful if we first begin to see clearly that our egoic nature is mostly a defense mechanism protecting us from life. If we can see these beliefs and defenses as simply layers of ego, simply impersonal defenses without any inherent Reality in them—if we can see that we do not need to defend ourselves from our friends, family and from life, everything changes and it becomes easy to let go. If we can reflect, for example, on our political opinions, we see that during election years everyone becomes so divided and polarized by their beliefs and opinions. As we join in this divisiveness, we create intense separation between those who are like us and those who will vote differently than us. We create wars in our minds, and a huge separation between us and them. To live in ego is to live in separation, yet we do not have to act this way. We can ask ourselves: *Do we need to fight with others? Do we need to constantly defend or attack? Do we need to stand on one side of the fence? Do we need to create this division?* What we discover is that all of this is unnecessary, and creates a tremendous amount of pain with each other. There is a different way to live. We may ask ourselves: *how would our world be different if we listened to each other and took care of each other, instead of fighting with or defending ourselves from each other?*

If we want to be free in this way, we find that it is helpful to examine each of the various layers of ego and investigate if there is any solid or fixed reality to any of them. We may start with the layer of ego made up of our mental thoughts. What we find is that our thoughts spontaneously and mysteriously arise in our minds. When we watch our thoughts, we can see that we don't even know what they are or where they come from—they just arise. They are a mysterious impersonal phenomena, but we talk about them like they are real, as if they exist in reality. Then we identify with them and allow ourselves to be defined by this mysterious arising phenomena and assume for some reason that we *are* what we think. Yet, we have no real idea what thoughts actually *are*. They have no solid or material reality; they have no mass or weight, but many of us would give our lives to defend our thoughts. Many of us believe that we *are* our thoughts, and live without ever questioning this. But as we examine our thinking as it arises and subsides, what we find is that, if our thoughts were to totally disappear, that we would not disappear with them. What we are left with is pure seeing and direct experiencing. But if we take thoughts to be real and begin to believe in their divisive nature, we suffer. Essentially our ego is made up of thoughts and psychological forces; as long as we take this to be us, we will miss the freedom that we are, when we allow ourselves to be simply the pure seeing of our experience.

If we look deeper and see through the movement of thought, what we may find next is emotion. What are emotions, we may wonder? Is there anything permanent, fixed, or solid about emotions? We find that emotions are deeply *felt* thoughts or beliefs. Often because of the strong sensations that go along with emotions, we believe feelings actually *mean* something, but we find that if we do not assign a meaning to our feelings, they mean nothing and quickly disappear. It is not until we *assign* a meaning to the feeling that we really *care* about it. I have often experienced the feeling of heartache and the thought pattern that normally goes with this feeling: *if she would come back then I could be happy*. But if I do not *give* any meaning to the emotion of heartache, then the feeling quickly passes. If no meaning is assigned, feelings simply arise and fall within our consciousness effortlessly and we *feel* what's here, but do not suffer; we suffer when we argue with what is here. We suffer when we don't want certain feelings to arise and want other feelings to stay longer. To wake up out of unconsciously assigning meanings to our feelings, it is helpful to examine the stories we assign to our feelings. Often our emotions are connected to some story of the past or future. But if we see that this story is simply a story with no inherent reality outside of our minds through inquiring into our assumed or perceived judgment of reality, the stories quickly fall apart. As our stories fall apart our emotions quickly begin to deflate or release, if we are willing to courageously feel them and experience them directly.

To allow for this process of emotional deflation or release, it can be helpful to simply experience emotions in their most basic essence, *as movements of energy*. If we take a deep look at emotion, we find that beyond the thoughts and stories that are attached to our emotions, that they are simply sensations moving through our bodies. Not many individuals have been trained to look or question what is arising within them. Instead most individuals simply react to these movements of sensation within them, without ever taking the time to investigate these movements of feeling that so radically affect our lives. *What are sensations,* we may ask? Upon deeper examination we find that sensations are, in their most basic form, simply movements of energy. Yet we will often make our major life choices based on these feelings and energies. We may ask, *is there any inherent or absolute truth to the meanings that we have assigned to our emotions? Do we know that our assumptions based on our feelings are absolutely true?* Through questioning our emotionally based assumptions or conclusions we have made about life, we can become free to see what is truly here. It takes a courageous individual to question themselves at every level of their being and it is only through this type of thorough investigation, will we become free at each level of our existence.

Beyond questioning the conclusions about life that we draw based on our emotionality, we can inquire deeper within at the level of our identity. We may ask, *are we our emotions? What are emotions? What are emotions energetically?* We can examine the emotional sensations that arise within us by asking, *is there anything solid or permanent about these sensations? If we allowed a surgeon to operate on us, would they be able to extract the emotions or feelings? Or are they simply phenomena also? Can we exist without them?* Many of us believe that we are our emotions, but *are we not here when they come and when they are gone? What is this that witnesses the coming and going of thought and emotion? Are we not that, which witnesses our temporary thoughts and emotional experiences?*

In the Zen tradition, we are instructed to investigate into *what is permanent about us*, while inquiring into who we *actually* are beyond our fleeting egoic nature. Because emotions and thoughts come and go, they cannot be us, for we are here to see them arise and to see them go. We are that which *sees*. This is so incredibly obvious, yet we miss this because the pull of ego entrances us into believing that we are the movement of these psychological forces. But we have a *choice* where to identify. If we put our attention on that which *sees* the movement of mind, we become the ever present witness. Or if we put our attention on what we think and feel, we then identify with that and we become the contents of our minds. When we discover this, we discover that we have the freedom to be lost in thought and feeling or to wake up out of thought and feeling and into spacious Awareness as ourselves.

The Buddha said that emotions and thoughts are empty. By this, he meant they have no solid tangible substance, yet in our experience we notice that emotions have a feeling behind them. As we investigate deeper and deeper into the emotional layer of ego and peel it away, piece-by-piece, layer-by-layer, we end up finding nothing solid, permanent or real—simply more layers of energetic phenomena arising in spaciousness. The only thing permanent we find in us is a spacious emptiness and a pure seeing and experiencing of everything that arises. Everything else seems to be an impermanent coming and going phenomena. Most of us have spent our whole lives lost in ego defending our perceived self that is essentially an *arising phenomena with no inherent reality*. When we wake up, we experience the beauty of knowing that we are not our egos, that we are *no thing*. When we can be this humble, this open, a funny thing happens; we become everything. We become everything because there are no longer walls defining us. We are not in the prison cell of our egoic definition of our self. When we see through our selves and find nothing solid and permanent there, we are free to be everything. As we look out at the world, what we see is us. We see that we are an awake, alive essence and that all of life is vibrating with this alive essence.

If we realize ourselves to be everywhere and everything, then what is there to defend? We can relax, because we no longer have to defend *our* point of view from *that* point of view. We no longer have to be a democrat or a republican. We no longer have to fight against life. We no longer have to assert ourselves. We no longer have to be worthy or unworthy. We no longer have to be healed. We can just be our authentic selves without any need to defend because what we are doesn't need to be defended. As soon as we defend *this ego* we create a great duality; we create an *us* and a *them*. We become small and limited verses being huge, vast and inclusive. We become entranced in ego again; because how would it be possible to defend the vastness of everywhere or the emptiness of no thing? No thing and everything could not be defended, nor needs to be defended.

To bring this awakened view into a concrete practicality, we might ask, *what would our life look like, if we were undefended?* I am certainly not recommending we become passive observers. But we may ask, what would our life look like if we stopped upholding, defending, and asserting our egos? We could still have our preferences and we still could vote. But while we stood in line to vote, we could be at Peace with life. We could be at Peace with other individuals with different views than ours and know them as our very Selves. Because when we wake up to the truth of what we are, we find that we are one with all of Life. We vote from what is true in our heart, and know there is no division between us and anyone. This is the beautiful thing that happens when we allow the walls of our ego to drop; we realize that we *are* all of Life. To be undefended does not mean we give up and do nothing. We still show up for life, we still go to work; but perhaps, we do not argue over petty things with our boss or coworkers. We will *choose* to live differently because we no longer care about petty differences, and instead give our attention to the vast perspective of oneness which is right here in our ordinary lives. When we live in this way, we discover that so much of what we thought to be worth fighting for is a waste of time and energy. And yet, we still assert ourselves where necessary. Gandhi gave a good fight, but his fight came from Peace and that is why he was so powerful. Martin Luther King Jr. had good fight within him, yet he was totally undefended. We see how powerful it is to be undefended because even though their lives have ended; their fight, their Peace carried on and changed the world. By being undefended, we give ourselves and those around us the gift of freedom. So this is our constant ongoing invitation: to choose now to live with no defense. This means we choose to be undefended even when the defenses habitually arise; we love, allow and embrace every aspect of ourselves, which creates an ongoing environment for our own defenses to let their guard down and truly let go. As we actively choose not to defend our egoic nature, in doing so, we become the movement of evolution and Love itself, which is naturally here, when we begin to live beyond our habitual egoic nature.

You Are Enough

For thousands of years, saints and sages have said that happiness is within. However, when most of us settle down from our busy lives and begin to look inside, what we find is a swirl of emotions and pain that we have been avoiding, and a stream of conflicting thoughts that drives us fairly crazy. "Where is the inner peace and happiness," we may ask? In this brief moment after asking this question, is where most of us make our mistake. Instead of taking the time to deeply investigate within (which requires that we are patient enough to take the time to see through the pain and insanity of our minds and discovering this depth within that is beyond our momentary suffering), we impatiently give up our inward search and look to the outside world again for happiness. But after searching for and failing to find lasting happiness in the external world, we again look inward and again are met with our own pain and confusion. Many of us spend lifetimes, going between these two shallow worlds of seeking pleasure and avoiding pain, often lost and confused. "Is it actually true," one may ask, "is there lasting happiness and contentment within? And if so, how does one find this elusive inner Peace and happiness?"

As a counselor and spiritual teacher, I sometimes think of myself as in the pain and peace business. Pain normally brings us to search for a deeper relationship to life. It wasn't until I was in so much pain and confusion that I got serious about the spiritual path and for most of us this seems to be the case. Over the years, I have met many who struggle with pain or who are searching for inner peace, and these two of course, are deeply and paradoxically connected. I often ask individuals where they find peace and happiness. Most point to the heart as the seat of peace and happiness. But when we inquiry deeper, often what I find is that, when I guide someone through meditation to come into their heart to experience this inner happiness, a bizarre thing for them happens. Often fear or anger or sadness arises and they even sometimes turn pale and want to end this experience as quickly as possible. Because of this frightening experience, often they make the assumption that what they *are* is somehow flawed or broken or not pure. I smile, because I know this experience well. Many of us mistake the pain and emotions that lay on top of the heart, for our heart. When we misperceive the pain of our emotions as our heart, as the place where we would expect to find our deep peace and contentment, we mistakenly choose to want nothing to do with our hearts. This is sadly, why so many of us stay as far from our hearts as possible. Unfortunately, most of us do not actively inhabit our hearts, because they are too covered in pain; we instead take refuge in our thinking minds and all of its defenses and avoidance strategies. This dance of avoiding our pain, fuels our egoic illusion. But in our thinking minds there is no satisfaction either, because for most of us our minds are very much neurotic, irrational and spinning out of control. If we take refuge in thoughts, then we are at the mercy of whatever thoughts arise. Much of our suffering comes from identifying with either arising thoughts or painful emotions as who and what we are. This dance is the fundamental misperception that fuels our suffering.

So what are we doing wrong here, we may ask? It comes from a fundamental error that we all make. When we go inward, we look at the contents of our mind and emotions for our happiness. When we see or feel these thoughts and emotions, we unconsciously identify with them. This is similar to walking into a movie theater and believing that we are part of the drama on the screen, instead of knowing that we are the witness to what happens on the screen. But we are not the drama that is unfolding; we are the *one* watching the movie. We are the thing watching, experiencing, and registering the thoughts, emotions, and stimulus. We are the field of awareness and have always been the field of awareness. And all of life, with all of its pain and beauty arises in this field of awareness. If we make the mistake of identifying with what arises, then we will suffer because of our attachment to it or from our resistance of what comes and goes. We basically want what feels good to last longer and what is painful to leave us immediately; this is the dance of our dualistic egoic mind. As long as we are identified here, we will be lost in the pain of samsara—the pain of our minds.

But deep within us, we *know* that we are not what we see or experience arising; that is why we continue to look for a peace that cannot be affected by the coming and goings of life. When we go to the theater, we have to actively *suspend our disbelief* to begin to believe in the drama of the movie, to be able to enjoy it, to experience it. We have to agree to take the movie to be *reality*, but something deeper in us knows that the movie is just a movie. When we are fully in the *dream state* of the movie, and a monster jumps out, we scream. This is what it means to be dreaming or unconscious in a spiritual sense; we believe the thoughts and emotions that arise in us and take them to be a clear representation of reality, instead of seeing them as a lens that distorts Reality or as something that has nothing to do with Reality. What makes being clear or awake to our true nature even more difficult is that built into our ego is an unconscious drive to *suspend our disbelief* when it comes to our *own* thoughts and emotions. As our thoughts and emotions arise on the screen of our consciousness, we dream automatically. We unconsciously believe our thoughts, mostly without questioning their validity or truth. It happens automatically and this is why so many of us are asleep at the wheel, at the mercy of what we think and feel. As we believe in what we think and feel, the ego is busy creating a sense of self and a sense of reality, and a sense of temporary happiness or unhappiness that we become lost in.

We have the *dream state* wired into our egoic consciousness. For most of humanity, it is very difficult to wake up out of this unconscious mechanism that suspends our disbelief in relation to thought, emotion, and stimulus. Because our ego automatically suspends our disbelief, we habitually take thought and feeling to be *our self*, to be who we are. But let us take another look at who we are. It is so obvious and elusive, that we rarely even notice what we are. If we sit in a movie, and know that we are not the characters on the screen, then what are we? We are, of course, the one that *is doing the seeing*; we are *awareness*. We cannot be our thoughts or emotions because we can experience them arise within us. What is present is thoughts and emotions, and the one that *sees* thoughts and emotions. We are the one who sees what arises within us. We could not be the thoughts and emotions because they are always emerging, changing and disappearing into the space of our consciousness.

If we want to be deeply happy in the way sages have spoken about for thousands of years, then as we look inward, we must allow ourselves to become *aware* of awareness. To see this, we have to direct our attention to the alive space of ourselves. We have to allow the one who sees, to turn around and see oneself. We have to allow awareness to turn upon itself and see itself. As we do this, we begin to see and directly experience ourselves as Luminous Awareness. To do this, we do not put our awareness on our thoughts or our emotions; this is the fundamental error. We look at what is *seeing* the thoughts and *experiencing* the feelings. We realize that we are the watcher and the space beyond the watcher, and that what we are is vast, luminous, mysterious, fully perfect and complete; and there within this space thoughts and feelings arise. As we step into the Reality of ourselves, we experience ourselves as such a deep well of Peace, happiness and contentment, that it makes any fleeting egoic happiness nothing in comparison to that which we are.

Another common and habitual error we may experience while looking inward, is to think that we *are* our experiences. This again is a misperception and fuels spiritual seeking. If we practice yoga and feel blissful, we mistakenly think that our true self is the experience of Bliss and that if we could hold onto this bliss and somehow prolong it, then we would be happy. This can be confusing because as we step into our true self, we tend to feel Bliss. But the true self is not the *feeling* of Bliss. The true self is not a feeling. How could who and what we are be a feeling? If the true self were a feeling, the true self would be as fleeting, fickle, and elusive as feelings are. The true self is the one who *experiences* the feeling, not the experience. What we are *truly* is not dependent upon good feelings or positive thoughts or certain spiritual states or experiences. The true self is beyond thoughts, beyond feelings, beyond experiences. It has to be; thoughts, feelings, and experiences come and go. Who we are does not come and go.

We are here and have always been here as the *seeing*. Again, our true self is the one that sees, the one that feels, the one that experiences, the *very space* in which this all takes place; not the actual feelings, thoughts, and experiences. To be awake means we know and realize this, not intellectually, but as who and what we truly are. After 14 years of intense seeking I realized this and it came with an incredible opening, a *Satori,* or moment of clear seeing, one dreadful afternoon. I was suffering greatly and in so much pain, that I gave up trying to figure out and control life with my mind. As I let go, out of a feeling of despair from being both totally exhausted with my mind and being completely emotionally defeated, my ego collapsed into itself. An explosion of energy began to tremble through my being. I began to laugh so hard that I thought I would pull a muscle and soon I was crying so hard that tears drenched my shirt. I fell to the floor and laughed and cried like a mad man. It was such an incredible relief to finally let go of trying to find anything true in my mind or emotions. And as I did, I began to wake up to Truth as me, not truth in my mind or thoughts—but I woke up to true seeing as me, as my very own Self.

Even after deeply realizing my True nature and living in the transcendent Reality for weeks, my ego came forward again and I unconsciously moved back in to the dream state, which came in the form of an *unconscious suspension of disbelief*. Instead of simply resting as the hugeness of awareness as myself, I again believed in my thoughts, feelings and experiences as my identity. The ego naturally comes forward and pulls us back out of the transcendent, not because it is inherently wrong or bad, but because it is constantly making sure that we practically function and take care of ourselves in the world. We still need to have *some* egoic functioning so that we remember to go to work and take care of our children. Some individuals have made grave decisions in the name of oneness and ended their jobs, relationships or parenting responsibilities, because they discovered *all is one*. It is true that *all is one*, but this does not mean we no longer have a practical life to show up for. After we wake up to the transcendent, the egoic identity comes forward again so that we will continue to take care of this form, and those around us: our children, our jobs, our families, our bodies. We do not need to fight the pull back into our ego; it is simply trying to make sure we are safe and taken care of the best way it knows how.

If we understand why this movement of mind is happening and use a *gentle discipline*, we can remain open to the transcendental Reality and remain practical. Gentle discipline means that we gently resist the temptation to believe *all* our thoughts or to assign meaning to them. We stay open by seeing thought as simply a movement of mind, with no inherent truth or meaning, and emotion as a movement of sensation that is not to be feared or pushed away. If we can see thought as *thought* and fully embrace the feeling of emotion without getting involved with the story of it, then life begins to move smoothly for us. In this openness, we allow emotion and thought to move through us without creating a great deal of suffering. And of course if our ego is reminding us that we need to eat or go to work, we naturally listen, because this is our ego doing its job in a healthy manner. If we work with our ego in this way, we can remain awake and allow for a practical integration of our ego. This process tends to be very messy for most of us, due to the strong pulls of our egoic mind and all the insecurity and rejected aspects of ourselves that are waiting to be loved, healed, and released or integrated.

Naturally, we often go back and forth from being awake to being lost in thought. At first, this may be extremely painful to go from being awake and experiencing oneself as all of life, to being lost in thought. Gradually though, awareness begins to solidify as our identity as we begin to choose to remain open, and to not be too involved in our thoughts and from this openness we can choose to *use* our minds, instead of being *used* by them. As a maturity develops within, we choose which thoughts to act upon and which to leave alone. We respond to life, instead of reacting to it; and an incredible intuitive intelligence begins to develop as we choose to stay open. Somewhere along the way a natural integration takes place, where we are free *of* our minds, yet able to use them when necessary.

However, most of us who wake up still have quite a bit of work to do. Even though we wake up out of identity with our egos or the movement of our minds, for many of us the ego is strong and there are still places where the ego has the power to pull us back into its unconscious identification. We usually struggle with our deepest shadows, pain, and parts of ourselves that we have denied and continue to deny. My teachers have reminded me that even after awakening and shifting our identity out of ego, that this process of discovery, deepening, and integration continues on forever and that we are always beginners. As beginners, we stumble again and again over our shadows and will continue to grow in our embodiment and Divinity. I find myself paradoxically overwhelmed by the depth of my experience of oneness and unity as my own self, while at the same time, I have to laugh at all the places where my humanity comes forward and I act like a fool while I continue to be deluded by my own ignorance.

The old teachings that *Maya* or the drama of everyday life is all illusion, works great if you live in a cave with disciples who feed and take care of you or if you have a large trust fund. A more inclusive view of Reality is that the world of form is Divine as well. As Ramana Maharshi, the great Indian Sage said, "The world is illusion, Brahman (God) alone is real, Brahman is the world." All is God. Somewhere along the way we realize this in the depth of our being and a very natural integration takes place. There is no longer the feeling of being awake and being asleep. We realize that we are always awake, and always *were* awake. We just were not aware of ourselves. We were lost in ego, continually suspending our disbelief, identifying with thought as our selves. As we continue to integrate into this new reality, even despite our unconscious movement of mind, we *know* that we are not the movement of our minds. We don't have to sit in meditation for 15 or 20 years to realize this. We don't have to wait lifetimes. We can simply and directly know who we are in this moment by becoming aware of awareness and surrendering to Life as ourselves.

We can experience this right now. As we slow down and take deep full breaths and unhook from our minds, we will begin to directly change our experience. As we go inward and witness the witness or turn awareness upon ourselves, what do we see? Are we vast? Are there no boundaries to ourselves? Are we quiet? Are we still? Are we vibrant and alive? Yes, we are already these. If we make the mistake of asking our minds to answer these questions, we will get a misrepresentation of ourselves. But when we turn around and see who we are, we see an awake, aware, vibrant Presence reading this very sentence.

Allowing life to be as it is

As we reflect deeply on what it means to be fully free in our life and in this world, we may notice that there are two main aspects of spiritual freedom. There is the freedom we experience *within* our self when we discover that we are not our conditioned and judgmental minds, but instead know ourselves to be a boundless, awake presence. Building upon this realization, there is the freedom of the sage who *gives* this boundless freedom to everyone and everything, fully loving and accepting life exactly how it is. We can see that the second stage or aspect of freedom is much more inclusive of the totality of life. Yet the first stage of freedom is a necessary step to this greater realization, in fact without the direct experience of this first stage we will always remain stuck in the delusion of our minds.

In the beginning stages of awakening, it is important and necessary for us to finally be able to see who we truly are beyond our mind and emotions. But it is not until one day later, that we discover that this is only one aspect of freedom. It would absolutely, be a huge evolutionary step forward for humanity, if we all could know and live from our true nature. Yet at some point in our journey, we may realize that despite the discovery of our own innate divinity that we have not yet given freedom to *the world*, for the world to be as it is. This is a deeper and more mature type of freedom, than simply knowing ourselves to be spaciousness.

Within a few minutes of inward investigation we will notice all the areas of our lives that we have not allowed life to be as it is. We may discover this arise when we come into contact with our parents or our partners or our boss. We may discover that our freedom is not fully inclusive and totally accepting when we experience feelings of agitation or irritability or deeper feelings of anger, jealously, or hurt in our everyday lives. As these feelings arise within us, it is human for us to begin to reidentify with our mind and the parts of us that haven't been fully transformed by the vast freedom that we are. This lack of freedom will be apparent to us, because we will be irritated with the world to some degree or another and when we are, we will see that part of us is still resisting life. For example, when visiting our parents or family during the holidays, we may notice that we may not feel as free as we did at the end of our long meditation retreat. This experience can be a blessing if we can see that the irritation within us has come forward, to show us where we have more work to do, where we are still not free. From this perspective of absolute openness, we can allow Life to show us all of the places where our egoic mind is still *wanting* life to be different than it is. To be fully free means we must be fully willing to see and accept life for what it is, without any argument or agenda for it to be different than it is. It is only when we let go this deeply will we actually be able to heal and transform our pain of the past and discover a freedom that has no end.

Yet To be deeply free in this way, we must be willing to allow everything to be as it is in each and every moment. This does not mean we are unresponsive to life, in fact we are much more likely to respond with love and compassion, if we have first accepted the causes, conditions and individuals in our current circumstance. On the other hand, if we still have spiritual arrogance then we will expect the whole world to do a song and dance around us so that our freedom is not disturbed. If this sounds like us, at some point we may find that we are still very much deluded, by our minds and emotions, despite experiencing some level of personal spiritual freedom. True freedom is not about having a wonderful and blissful never ending personal experience, although bliss is one of the many byproducts of awakening. With true freedom, our whole relationship to life changes; our orientation to life completely changes and our relationship to life is no longer just about what we *think* and *feel*. It is about a far greater movement. In fact, the more free we become, the more we see that freedom has nothing to do with the wants and desires of our ego. Egoic freedom is having all the wants and desires of our ego endlessly satisfied. But with true freedom, we stop believing that the wants and desires of our mind will actually make us happy and as we grow in this freedom, we begin to allow everyone and everything to be as they are.

We no longer ask the world to be this way or that way. We let everyone be who they are, without commenting about them or judging them, without putting them in a box of right or wrong. We give up all our agendas for those around us. When we surrender in this way, our whole energetic nervous system calms down and we discover that, it is such a relief to finally allow everything to be as it is, without any need for Life to be different.

When my son was a toddler, I often became frustrated with him for *being* a toddler. I would sit for hours and hours in meditation and he, being a toddler, would laugh and cry and throw balls against the wall where I was meditating and make all kinds of noise. When I was a young dad, I was the kind of spiritual guy who wanted the world to be quiet around me. But we cannot ask the whole world to be silent while we chase enlightenment. This is not freedom. If we ask the world to bend over backwards for us, so that we can maintain our private world of bliss—that is more like tyranny.

Unfortunately for my son, his new dad was a tyrant and he had to spend many of his years straightening me out. Noah and I started off our relationship with me wanting him to be quiet and him wanting to be a toddler doing what toddlers do. Of course, I did not win this battle. It took me many years to learn how to be a dad and even longer to learn to allow the world to be as it is. During this time I had to learn to relax, let go and that I was going to be absolutely fine without trying to micromanage others or the environment around me. I had to take the time to slow down and see that my wanting to control came from a deep insecurity in relationship to life. Over the years, I have made friends with this insecurity through sitting with it, listening to it, feeling it and breathing into it, without any need or desire to get rid of it. As I embraced my insecurity whole heartedly, it finally released. As it did, I noticed that I was able to relax and began to stop projecting this inner insecurity onto my outer life. If we want to be free, we will makes friends with the difficult places within and *love them to death*. This is our work and our ongoing invitation: to notice what is within us, where we resist life, and to meet it with love and allow this healing from the inside out, to change the very way we relate to life.

A wonderful joy can come to us and those around us, if we can be willing to allow everything to be as it is. But, if we try to control and argue with reality, we will lose almost every time. It is almost guaranteed that we will not be happy, if we want life to be different than it is. Imagine how much peace we would experience if we totally accepted our parents, our partners, and our children exactly as they are, without wanting or asking them to be different at all. This can be an incredibly powerful question for us to sit with. If we want to be free, we must be willing to question all of our expectations, assumptions and judgments about life and of those around us. We may sit with this question for some time, "What would our life be like if we totally accepted our parents, our partners, our children, anyone and everyone exactly the way they are without wanting them to be different in any way?" We know what life is like if we continue not accepting them. How would our life change if we let everyone be as they are?

I can remember when I first heard this question, "can you accept them completely?" from the spiritual teacher Eli Jaxon Bear. It was after years of spiritual practice and therapy; I was angry and hurt and struggling to forgive my family for being themselves. Even though I had a fairly good childhood comparatively, deep inside I was still furious. I had been struggling with this anger for years and yet one day, when I heard this question, I surrendered. I said *ok*, and in a fraction of a moment, everything dropped out of me, I no longer needed my family to be different. My God, what a relief it was, to allow them to be who they are, and to allow me to be me, without looking to them to be different, to change, or to see or validate me. What a relief it is if we allow others to be who they are. We may notice that once we allow others to be as they are, our relationships with them begins to take place in the present moment, instead of taking place in the projections of our minds where they need to first change before we will be open to them and able to listen to them. When we begin to live in this way, it is as if all of our relationships become brand new again, because for the first time in our lives, we are seeing who is in front of us without our projections of the past telling us what we see.

Letting go of control

If we examine our egos in a deep and honest way, we will find that the nature of the ego is much like a tyrant who wants to judge and control everyone and everything in our environment. Most of us do not hear the voice of this *inner tyrant* until something does not go our way. If someone challenges us at work, or asks us to turn down our music or takes our parking spot, we may discover our inner tyrant awakening from its slumber. With a few minutes of mindfulness, we may find ourselves shocked by this inner tyrant who is offering its opinion and judgment of life and of others on an almost constant basis. Many of us may discover this inner critic when we take some time to be in silence or in meditation. It can be quite humbling to consciously discover that we are not as "spiritual" as we thought we were. Yet, when we discover ourselves judging or criticizing it is simply an invitation to see, that an aspect of our mind is not seeing life clearly. And when we see this, it is an opportunity to ask, *why are we not seeing clearly?*

If we take some time to become curious why this tyrant exists within us, we may learn something about our psychological wiring and how this wiring influences how we relate to life. This is important because our psychological wiring or ego is the primary veil that covers our inherent freedom. If we meet this aspect of ourselves with loving kindness and we honestly *listen* to this aspect of our egoic selves, what we find is that within us is a deep insecurity and masking this insecurity is a vicious and yet helpless tyrant. If you haven't yet seen this inner tyrant in yourself, just put yourself in a situation where you do not have any control. You will soon find the mind going into panic, as it quickly tries to regain a *sense* of control in this wild world. Our ego is inherently insecure because deep in our core we know that life is absolutely unpredictable and uncontrollable. In fact our ego is essentially a defense mechanism created by evolution to help us react to the wild nature of this world.

When we are mindful, we discover that this insecurity is greatly exasperated when faced with the unpredictable and uncontrollable nature of Reality. Although most of the time, because we are so deeply identified with our egos, we do not actually see this dance of ego arising with us, because we righteously and unconsciously believe that we *know* how life should be. This is essentially the pain of samsara; the pain of being lost in our own insecure and yet, arrogant minds. Yet here lies the doorway to our freedom, if we can relax into this vast insecurity and meet our minds with love, we become free. But not many of us are willing to relax in the face of the absolute insecurity of life. Most of us will run back to the security of our repetitive habits or mentality and meet life, from a defensive, attacking or grasping stance—as long as we go back to the security of our past egoic tendencies, we will not grow, but continue to repeat the past and continue to live in suffering. To be free we must choose to break ourselves from the habitual nature of our minds, and relax in the great insecurity with a willingness to respond to life from Love. To do this requires that we become fully conscious of ourselves through slowing down, breathing, and then consciously responding, instead of simply reacting.

As we sit deeply with our egoic consciousness, we find that one of the primary ways the ego deals with this inherent insecurity of life is to try to control the environment for the sake of our own personal or psychological safety. When we don't feel in control, our mind's habitual response is to desperately seek to control life or those around us in order to regain a sense of security. The felt experience of this insecurity is the feeling of panic or anxiety. We may think that this is an exaggeration, but in countless therapy sessions, I have seen individuals willing to end a marriage or relationship because they were not getting their way. Of course, it is easy for us to see this behavior in others, yet if we are honest we have all been guilty of being a tyrant. I can remember when I was younger, that I refused to go on vacation once, because I would not be in control of my time or where we would eat our meals. My inner tyrant was willing to give up a wonderful vacation, because it may not have been able to control every aspect of the vacation; how foolish, I was. We humans bicker and fight over the most insignificant things and all the while miss the wonderful love and unity that is available to us, when we don't have an agenda and can relax into the wonder of this present moment.

If we want to be free, we must be willing to become comfortable with not being in control and without manipulating others for our own desires. This means being willing to breath and relax when we do not get our way. It means being willing to breathe and relax when our mind is spinning and feeling unsettled and creating wonderful arguments of why our way is the correct or is the only way of doing things. To be free means we need to be comfortable with Life doing her dance around us, without us going into panic or making a scene if things are not exactly our way. We know that Life can be quite wild and unpredictable; at any moment, we or those around us could lose our jobs or our partner, get in an accident, or inherit great wealth. To be free in this world requires that we can allow everything to be as it is and yet be fully awake to respond to life with love.

Ironically, if we have faith in our mind's ability to control and manipulate life, we will *assume* an artificial sense of being in control and *feel* safe as a result, but this perceived safety is simply an empty mask sitting on top of an ocean of insecurity. But if we want to be free, we let go of this false mask or assumption and look closely at who and what we are beyond our minds. When we see through our egoic masks, and see that it is simply a movement of arising phenomena and inherently empty of any solid, stable self; then we can realize that we do not need to protect this mask; we do not need to protect our movement of thoughts, ideas, agendas, opinions, and desires. When we see that we are the one who sees, not the contents of our mind, which make up the mask, we realize that there is no one here that needs to be protected. If we can see that our ego is simply a movement of insecure mental phenomena, we see that we do not need to protect it, because what would be the point of protecting a mask, an image. If we can instead see that we are not the mask, but the one who simply sees life with or without a mask, if we can realize that this one who is *aware* must be who we are then we can be free.

If we investigate this awareness, what we find is that the one who sees is already complete, whole, total, vast, and indestructible. The *seer* is here no matter what unfolds in life and when we know this in our core, that we are the *seer* who is always simply seeing life no matter what comes our way, then we realize that the *seer* cannot be harmed. Our masks, our identities, our ideas, opinions and political beliefs on the other hand, most certainly can be harmed if we believe in them and think that we need them to be happy or for a sense of identity. However if we discover ourselves to be *that which is beyond our minds*, then we know that if our mask is harmed by life, we still live on as the one who simply witnesses the movement of life whether it is good or bad, painful or blissful.

Imagine if we identify deeply with our political party and our candidate does not win the election, then we suffer. But if we identify as the *seer*, then it does not matter from an absolute perspective who wins, even though in a relative way (from the perspective of our personal nature), we may have a preference for *this* or *that*. Yet over time, we can realize that we will be fine if we allow our protective walls to drop and do not get our way, and as a result of this letting go, we will naturally, not try to force everyone around us to be like us or act in accordance with our egoic need for control so that we can feel safe. Since most likely, what we are doing when we are protecting and trying to control is an egoic defense against a perceived or assumed fear, this preemptive movement of mind is often very unnecessary. Now, in no way am I suggesting that we do not protect ourselves in difficult or dangerous situations—of course, we do this. There are many instances also, that we have a responsibility toward someone or something or have children. But often we can find within ourselves many moments when our mind has an insistence on controlling the outside world for its own benefit or egocentrism or because there is a projected fear that the past will repeat itself. If we give into this movement of controlling life when there is no real danger, what we are doing is living in an unconscious or deluded way and perpetuating our dream.

Letting go of our perceived sense of control can be quite difficult, especially if we have experienced trauma or abuse. Even long after, the trauma or abuse has occurred our ego will still want to maintain walls to protect itself against an often absent enemy. Even after we have rediscovered a practical sense of safety in our lives again, our ego can still find itself stuck in the past moment of danger. Though if we are mindful, we will see that there is nothing present that we need protection from and now, we can begin to allow our walls to drop and live in the beauty of the present spacious moment.

If we can realize that we are actually quite ok in this moment, we can relax and take the time to heal the trauma of our past. We do this by bringing our loving attention to the very aspect of ourselves which is still living in pain or insecurity. By meeting ourselves with a total loving kindness, this pain will eventually release from our being. After we take the time to fully heal our pain and insecurity, we can begin to give freedom to the world to be as it is in the present moment, without the need to control or fight with it. It is a tremendous act of courage to love the very aspects of ourselves that are hurting. As we love in this way, we discover that we are capable of fearlessly loving *anything*, because we are no longer only loving what feels good, but instead loving whatever arises within our experience. As we take the time to love this deeply we become Love, Itself. In the end we discover that our relationship with life does not become free from living behind walls or needing the world to be a certain way for us. It comes from realizing that there is nothing to protect and everything to love.

Is there a permanent solid self?

When the Buddha was asked if there was a self or not, he did not answer. He remained silent. For thousands of years there has been a great debate in the spiritual community with regard to the philosophy of self or no self, and although there are many arguments for and against, the original teachings of the Buddha conclude that there is *no permanent, solid, fixed self*. Yet most of us unconsciously assume the opposite, that there is a permanent and solid self that we refer to as *us*. But if we want to be free we must be willing to look deeply and see what is actually true within our experience. When we actually look inside, we somehow never find this solid and permanent self. No one seems to ever be able to produce this self upon investigation. We may wonder, where is this *self* in us? Of course there is *something* cognizant inside of us, but it certainly is not fixed or permanent or solid. The illusion of our mind is that it assumes the movement of thoughts and psychological forces are *true*, instead of seeing this movement as simply being an impersonal movement of mind (with no inherent solid Truth). This false assumption creates the illusion of a permanent, solid self.

If we can give ourselves permission in this very moment to stop believing in this movement of mind as the truth of reality, or stop being convinced by this unexamined, self-fabricated and imagined self, what are we left with? What is here when we stop believing our thoughts to be ourselves? What is here? Can we be so *humble* to stop and look right now? What do we notice that is here beyond our thoughts; is there not a simple conscious awareness? And is not this conscious awareness spacious, luminous, and silent? Can we notice how our awareness is directly experienced energetically throughout our entire being right here in this moment? Is this awareness still and vast? Is our awake, aware, still presence always here, even when we are thinking? Most people would say no that their thoughts are here. But don't our thoughts actually arise out of this space of Silence? See for yourself. What is the space that thoughts arise out of? Is it not silent, spacious Awareness and is this not absolutely beautiful, perfect and complete? This Awareness, therefore, must be who we are, because it is the only stable aspect of who and what we are. If we can deeply discover this, our life will dramatically shift in a wonderful way.

Buddhism teaches us that everything is impermanent. This wisdom, if investigated within relationship to our sense of self or sense of identity can help us to wake up out of our assumptions about who and what we think we are. It is easy to understand that all of us will one day die; it would be hard to argue with that. But if we examine the teachings on impermanence in relationship to our perceived self image and the building blocks of self image (mind and ego), the investigation comes closer to home. For example, our thoughts come and go; nothing in them is permanent. Some stay longer, but ultimately they all go. If we are looking for a permanent self, we have to look a little deeper and see what we find. When we look deeper, we see that our thoughts come and go and every emotion we ever had has come and gone. So what is here all the time? Silence is here all the time. A vibrant, alive, spacious, conscious Silence is here all the time. This Silence must be what we are; it is the only permanence of us—a spacious, silent, open awareness. All of our thoughts, emotions, and psychological forces arise out of this silent awareness, which we are. This means that we don't have to go anywhere to find ourselves. We simply have to see who we are, and who we are not. We don't have to travel to India to discover it. We just have to stop chasing and believing all the silly ideas and opinions of our own mind. Freedom is nothing that we get; it is actually a giving up of all of our identities, our seriousness, our charmingness, or whatever identity we have attached to in this lifetime. If we want to be free, we have to give it all up or let it be taken away by our vast presence allowing it to fall into our spaciousness. In the end, if we want to be free, we have to give up our identification with our imagined self and be what we have always been this entire time: the vast and luminous light of silent, spacious Awareness.

No problem

When we wake up out of the insanity of our minds, we realize that there is no problem with life. We realize that there are only situations in life. Some situations are painful and others are easy, but no situation is actually a *problem* until we decide in our minds that it is. This radical orientation only becomes possible, if we are willing to not believe in what we think. Because when we don't believe in the comments and the judgments that our minds tell us about life, it is impossible to have a problem; we simply and directly *see* and experience what is happening, right here, right now. If for example, it is cold outside—*it is simply cold*; there is no problem until we believe the thought in our mind that says, "*I don't like the cold.*" If our partner or boss criticizes us in some way, there is no problem—someone is simply expressing their opinion to us, and we have the opportunity to *choose* to respond to their comments, leave the situation, or simply let it pass by. There is actually no inherent problem in what they are telling us; we only suffer and have a problem if we believe their thoughts, and argue with them or start judging ourselves as a result. There are no real problems in what people do or say to us, until we decide that there are. When we wake up, we realize that we do not have to listen to anything that our mind says or what anyone says to us. We don't have to believe in their dream of reality or ours. We are free to simply *see, hear* and *feel* without believing in anyone's thoughts or our own about what we see, hear and feel. Knowing this *is knowing freedom* and only becomes possible from taking this teaching to the perspective of *absolute* truth. In absolute truth everything is simply as it is. Anything our mind has to say about life or our experience is a relative truth and can be debated. To be free requires that we step into the absolute truth that comes from simply seeing, hearing and feeling what is in front of us. If we are required to respond to any situation whether it is blissful or painful or difficult, we can choose to respond from the Truth or Love of the Divinity that we are. If we choose to instead see life as a problem and respond from our egoic defense system we will continue to live as a victim in this world.

If we investigate this deeper, what we find is that who and what we *are* simply *sees* and *experiences* life with a perfect acceptance and equanimity, yet meanwhile we have these minds that are layered on top of our essential nature that are constantly commenting on and criticizing life, always on the lookout for the next problem. Because of this dance, our minds habitually and neurotically make life a problem and we then identify as the victim of life. In the most practical sense, our minds are a defense mechanism that protects us from the dangers of life. But when there is no danger our mind begins to criticize ourselves or others simply out of the habit of looking for problems. Yet if we allow ourselves to slow down, to breathe and simply see what is in front of us, then the mental and emotional anxiety that our minds create out of a habitual defending against and fighting with life, can relax and release from our nervous system. When we calm down, we begin to see that there are situations in life that need to be addressed— not problems that we need to unconsciously defend ourselves against.

Of course, it would be foolish to deny that there is tremendous pain and suffering in the world, but from the radical perspective of being free, there is no problem; there is simply what is arising and this may or may not be comfortable. Divorce, surgery, heartache, illness, humiliation all may be quite painful, but pain does not have to be a *problem*. Pain is an experience we have in life; we may or may not be able to do something practically about it. But the very thought or perspective that life is a problem comes from our mind. The mind is wired to search for problems and danger constantly in order to protect us from harm. Yet if we let go of the perspective that life is a problem, we will see Reality simply as it is. Reality is here all the time, waiting for us to wake up to its rawness and beauty, waiting for us to step out of our mind, out of our limited perspective and waiting for us to directly experience the aliveness and wonder of Life. If we can see Life simply as it is, without seeing it through any filter of the mind, we will wake up to a wonderful, vibrant, intimate Reality. When we are willing to walk into this experience directly, what we will experience is unimaginable Unity—a Unity so vast it will make no sense to our egoic minds. On numerous occasions, I have found myself in unbearable mental, emotional and physical pain and yet, as I sat with this pain and fully embraced it with all of my being, this very pain transformed into *absolute bliss*. To our minds this statement seems like total nonsense, but when we step into Unity Consciousness boundaries dissolve, worlds collide and the unimaginable becomes normal.

To surrender this deeply takes a deep trust in life. Most of us instead, are plagued with a negative outlook on life based on our past experiences of mental, emotional and physical pain. These critical and pessimistic beliefs show up in our projections and judgments of life, of ourselves and of each other. A common experience for most of us is to not see clearly who our parents are. Many of us have had the bizarre experience of, as adults, going home to our parents' house and noticing that as soon as we walk into their presence, we regress and act like children or teenagers again. This is because we have an intense projection of who they are, so much so that our sense of self can digress to that of a teenager in their presence. As their children, our mind was conditioned to see them as our caretakers, the ones who knew about life, who we looked to for love and who would discipline us. Through our perceptions of them, we created or fabricated a "reality" of who we think they are. This is our filter, but our filter may or may not be true. Any filter will distort the truth of what we are seeing, any filter will ultimately get in the way from us seeing in the present moment *who* they are. The reason this is so, is because all projections or filters are based on past experiences and associations, which means we are seeing life through the past. When we do this, we are not seeing reality and as a result, we will ultimately experience a sense of separation and limitation from not engaging with what is actually here. Most of us continually see our parents (or anyone actually) through an outdated filter. These filters often have some unmet emotional need attached to it, which will cause us to see reality much differently than it actually is. We may unconsciously want them to love or treat us a certain way and when they don't, we get angry and suffer. Because we still have these unmet needs within us and are unconsciously expecting our parents to meet these needs, we continue to stay stuck in our past, waiting for them to give us the love that we are unwilling to discover within ourselves. We become free of our projections though healing the unmet needs within us with love and the willingness to step into the present moment and see that we are all that we need. As we heal this dance within us, we discover that our projections of our parents are no longer necessary and often no longer arise within us.

All these various filters that we have within us make life very much obscured. If we allowed our filters of ourselves to drop away and we saw our Divinity as who we really *are*, we would no longer look outside of ourselves for anything; we would find the complete perfection that we are in our innate Divinity right here, right now and always. Unfortunately, we have countless filters built into the fabric of our minds. Just as a photographer can put a filter on their camera lens, and distort the reality, our filters distort our reality. If we remove our filters, if we let go of them or stop believing in them and simply see life as it is, we will directly experience oneness and unity, and *see* and *experience* life clearly. In this clarity, we can allow others to be who they are without the need for them to be different. These egoic filters that arise in our consciousness do serve a purpose from an egoic perspective; they provide for us an artificial sense of security, because they help us to quickly put life in a box of *what's safe* and *what's not safe,* and helps us to organize life into manageable parts. But ultimately if we want to be free, we allow this unconscious movement of mind to drop out of us and realize that we do not need to put everyone and everything in a box. We realize that we will be just fine, without our preconceived way of seeing or being.

To let go of our habitual and defensive filters, it is very helpful to have a deep trust in the inherent goodness of life. When we trust in life it is easy to see that we don't need these protective layers of projection and judgment to defend us from this wonderful world. One of the most helpful skills we have is being able to breathe when life is difficult. If we are willing to slow down and breathe, we will begin to notice that no matter what the circumstances are, that we can relax into what is here in front of us. As we relax with whatever arises and see that whatever we experience, *we survive*, we begin to trust. We trust because we see that we (our essential nature) cannot be harmed no matter what experience we have or have had. When we discover this truth about life—that *we survive everything*, even our death, our orientation toward life shifts from *life is a problem that we need to defend ourselves from*, to trusting in the inherent goodness of ourselves and all of life.

I remember suffering a great deal as a young teenager from the confusion of teenage romance, which was my "problem" for years. On many evenings, I would get into my '73 Super Beetle and just go for a ride. I would turn the music up so loud that it would be impossible to think, and drive down some old county roads and look out at the stars, and began to open to the hugeness of Reality. I experienced the quiet and Beauty of the vast night sky and my blaring music. The music was my mantra—it kept my thinking mind busy. Yet, the direct experience was the vastness and Beauty of the sky and that life was perfect in some huge mysterious cosmic way. After these late night drives, I would come home and grab my dog and take him for a long walk in the fields. He was great because he did not stir up the drama or confusion in my mind; he would quietly and happily walk with me out into the vast night. My mind would spin off trying to understand life, or relationships, or try to understand the current drama in my life. My mind constantly recreated problems, where there were none, to no end. Ironically, I could never "figure" any of it out, and if I did figure anything out, my mind would simply present another problem to dwell on. And yet what I found was that the *vastness of the sky* was so much more seductive. My soul couldn't wait for me to walk darker and darker into the night.

Awakening can be seductive like a gentle pull into the vastness of the sky. Ironically, delusion can also gently pull us back into itself. I know on countless occasions, I have been pulled out of the vastness of the existence and into the incredible and sometimes endless drama of human relationship. Sometimes it can be a simple misperception of what was said that brings us back into the land of ego, or a major situation. All of these moments, when we are pulled back into delusion, are times when we can thank delusion for showing us again another place where we are not seeing clearly. I have seen this dance in so many ways within myself. Because I am divorced and co-parent with my former partner, there have been many times when I got pulled back into the confusing and painful filters of my past, but all of these have been opportunities for me to let go of a projection or an old belief system and step into the present moment of trying to work together with another incarnation of the Divine. The pull of delusion is not in any way bad or something to be avoided; it is here to teach us. Because Reality and delusion are one, they are *not* two opposing forces, they work together. Sometimes it takes us a long time to realize this. We all love the hugeness and clarity of the night sky, but delusion is also the intelligence of the universe waking us up in all the places we are still sleeping. When we discover this, nothing is any longer a problem; it is simply another invitation for us to Love in a deeper way.

Beyond Unconsciousness

One afternoon many years ago, I found myself listening to a show with interviews of many spiritual Masters and their students. As I listened to the stories of these great awakened ones, I began to wonder, *what is the difference between being awake and being a Master* or, put a different way, *what is the difference between being awake and being enlightened?* It felt at that time that I had experienced a powerful and profound awakening, but I noticed that I was not living up to the Truth of my direct experience in my daily life. I had become comfortable living in the experience of the transcendent reality, and yet in my everyday life, in the world of relationships and work I was coasting in many unconscious ways. I was full of an amazing transcendent bliss, yet staying very comfortable in *my world* and not really engaging life. I could see that my inner life was rich and wonderful; my mind, emotions and desires had greatly calmed. Fortunately, I was not getting in nearly as much trouble as I did in the past, yet something was still missing within me. As I sat with this feeling and began to examine my life, I saw that what I was missing was *embodying* this transcendent truth that I had realized. With many of the teachers that I have studied with, it seemed as if they had two qualities that most of us lack: their actions followed their words and they were no longer fooled by their own minds. And the more I looked at my life and my relationships, I began to humbly notice that time and time again, I was not living up to what I had realized.

When I was deeply honest, I saw that I had a great deal of work to do in these departments. What I was discovering is that the habits of the mind are deep and when it comes to my outward expression of my inner divinity, I (like many others) often habitually choose to live from the conditioned nature of our past. This dance leads to the confusing experience of feeling and experiencing great freedom, while also being drawn back into the habitual nature of mind. As a teacher, I meet more and more individuals who are having deep spiritual experiences and yet still remain deeply entranced in their own personal delusion. I can only have compassion for this, because it is something that we all struggle with. Throughout my day, I find so many occurrences when I am not seeing clearly and have to laugh at how confusing it can be to be both human and divine. A few years ago as we got closer to 2012, I saw my Armageddon thoughts increase substantially and sometimes, I got carried away by those thoughts. As I did, I could only laugh at myself and my thoughts of the apocalypse that never came. It can be quite confusing for someone to be on the path and wake up to a vast perspective of beauty, oneness and radiance—and then to lose that vision, and again struggle with the limited perspective of our habitual minds. Many deeply struggle with this experience of awakening and then being deluded again, and then experience a huge feeling of loss, as they find themselves being lost again in their mind's dream. Life even can be more painful, when we wake up to the ultimate Reality, and then find ourselves back where we used to be in the dance of suffering, because now we know what life *can* be like when we are living beyond the insanity of our minds.

However it is important to remember that this dance is completely normal and is part of the process of growing into our embodied divinity. We don't need to be that hard on ourselves when we fall, because we are all human. Even the Gurus and Masters, they too are human. Any great spiritual Master or Teacher can fall off the path or make painful mistakes like sleeping with their students, having affairs, or becoming power hungry—because they too are human. For years, I have put the great ones on a pedestal and it wasn't until I realized that they are human as well, that I understood that anyone can make a mistake or become deluded. Because we are all human, we all have minds with habitual thoughts and desires and cultural conditioning. When we wake up, sometimes our egoic conditioning disappears either permanently or temporarily. Yet, because we are all plugged into the collective consciousness, this conditioned habitual nature can come forward in any of us at any time, and when it does, we might be fooled into acting habitually or unconsciously in relationship to life. If we are honest, we can see that every way in which we are deluded comes from misinterpreting our thoughts as Reality. Luckily for us, awakening goes hand in hand with clarity and honesty. Awakening requires that we see clearly which means we have to be completely honest, otherwise we will again find ourselves deluded. Because being honest is seeing clearly, and anywhere where we are not being honest the pressure of awakening will push against us until whatever untruth is in the way begins to give way to a greater clarity and honesty. If there is anything that we can do to come into alignment with this honesty, it is to offer a courageous willingness to look, to examine, and to question our tightly held beliefs, desires and assumptions about our perceived reality and ourselves.

Ultimately there is only one human mind and all of us have this mind. In this mind lives all of the various thoughts of our collective consciousness: from fight and flight, to wanting to have a family, to desiring more power or control, and every other imaginable thought. Because of this, all of us can fall prey at any moment to being deluded by any movement of our minds and to mistaking our thoughts for Reality. When we wake up, we see clearly the nature of things; we see clearly the nature of the mind. This does not mean that all delusion will disappear from our being. The very programs of the human collective consciousness are in our biology: fight and flight, desire, anger, jealously, and all forms of ignorance. When we wake up, we gain a vast perspective, but this does not mean that these drives spontaneously and completely disappear from our being permanently and forever. Some of these programs we transcend, some dissolve, and many of these drives stay within us for the rest of our lives, unless we begin to work with them in a deep way, or they are spontaneously removed from our system by Grace.

Often with a powerful awakening or shift in perspective, various programs of the ego simply fall away; this is one of the wonderful graces of awakening. Yet for most individuals who experience a temporary shift, much of the ego (if not all of it) remains untouched and as the initial awakened perspective fades, delusion creeps back in its place. But what waking up gives us is a wonderful new space or perspective to work with delusion from the outside, instead of being stuck in it and trying to fix or heal our ego *with our ego*. To have this vast perspective stay vast or become more permanent, we must be willing to surrender completely to it and resist the temptation to believe what we think. This temptation is precisely how we unenlighten ourselves—by believing the stories in our heads. This can happen to anyone who believes the next thought that is not the truth, whether they are a Master Being or simply us. I know many individuals, myself included, who have been lost in the story of the coming of the end of our world. We have had this story deeply wired into our culture, even before biblical time. That is why when we work with thoughts on a collective consciousness level, they may require a greater level of willingness to be seen through or liberated from our consciousness. Even if the thought is objectively absurd, if the thought is wired into our collective consciousness it will require a deep examination and inquiry of it for us to let it go. This is what the spiritual path is all about—letting go of our past conditioning, letting go of who we are *not* and stepping into the present moment as the truth that we are.

Our challenge is always to live up to our realization; to walk the razor's edge of freedom means to not give into the habitual nature of our mind. This means that we resist the temptation of taking our thoughts and feelings to be true; to be Reality. It is a big job to live up to our realization and not to give into egoic games or programs. If we are going to walk this razor's edge, we do not do this from the self-righteousness of the ego; it has to come from the sincerity, strength and humility of our True Self, otherwise it will be just another movement we are deluded by. So this is our challenge, can we embody the Truth of who we are as us, instead of embodying the past as us, instead of embodying an unconscious habit of mind as us? Can we give ourselves to this and allow the Truth to live us, as Us?

Truth

Truth. Just the sound of it makes the mind stop. It is cold, silent, and clear, like the full moon shining on a lake. People often wonder what the *truth is* of a given situation. Yet if we want to know—we simply have to be courageous enough to ask our hearts. If we want to hear an argument or an intellectual dissertation, we can ask the mind. It will give us a long argument with many reasons why we are right, or why *this* or *that* is true. But when we ask our hearts, the answer is simple, quiet, and clear.

I can remember talking to some friends about what to do about a difficult decision in my life. All of my friends had a different idea for me and were very convincing in their arguments. They had themselves convinced that they *knew* exactly how I should live my life. Sound familiar? It is a bit hilarious how seriously we humans take ourselves and our opinions to be. If we look at what opinions are, we see that they are just points of view—not the Truth. Opinions can be quickly created in a fraction of a second by our minds, but they often have little conscious Truth within them. Opinions arise out of our conditioned and unconscious experiences of the past and are often simply a projection of our points of view from this past.

Most of our opinions are assumed to be true by our egos and have never really been examined by anything deeper than our conditioned and habitual minds, which is exactly where they arise from. If we deeply reflect upon this, it is quite frightening that most of what we think is simply a projection of our past experiences based on how a certain thought registered or felt to our emotional minds and nervous systems. In addition to this, much of what we think was also given to us over time by our biology, culture, and parents. So when we use our minds to discern what is true, our minds will look to two main sources: our past experience of how life has been (or how we are told it is) and our psychological projections, neither of which are close in comparison to the Divine Truth that is ever-present, alive and unaffected by events or mental or emotional projections from the past.

We can see this clearly in the act of forgiveness. If we hold onto the past, no war would ever end, nothing would get resolved. Forgiveness brings us into the present moment and requires a letting go and stepping into a new way of seeing reality. If we find ourselves stuck, it is because we are continuing to look to the past as a way to defend ourselves from either the present moment or a feared future moment that may or may not exist. But forgiveness is like the sky, it is open, free and ever present. The sky holds onto nothing; it allows everything to come and go in the present and as a result, it does not suffer or argue or want life to be different than the way it is. We embody Truth by stepping into the present moment and being completely open and allowing whatever is arising to come and go in the space of Love. As we step into this present moment, we allow ourselves to be open in our hearts to an intelligence that is greater than our minds. If this intelligence moves us to act, we act. If it moves us to be silent, we are silent and ever listening for the Truth to lead us.

Yet, so many of us want to argue about what we think is true. But again, the Truth is not a point of view based on our past psychological projection—at least not the Truth that I am speaking about. The Truth that I am referring to is as big as the sky and as powerful as the sun. It needs no convincing; It simply is. But most of us do not know how to step into this Non Dual Reality or even how to listen to the voice of Truth within. Some of us even deny this silent voice of Truth when it comes forward and speaks to us. I can admit that many times I have denied the Truth within me, and listened instead to the convincing voice of my mind. We all know this experience of hearing the quiet voice of our heart telling us to go *this* way or *that* way and instead, we ignore it as we listen to the loud voice of our minds. So many of us, I have found, are afraid of what's True, because our minds are often not in alignment with the Truth. Often our minds want to go here or there chasing desires or holding onto the past. Our minds want to be anywhere but in the Truth; because in the presence of Truth, the mind really has nothing to do. It can't go on and on rambling, chasing, avoiding, creating drama, gossiping, or giving a dissertation about this or that. When the Truth is present, the mind goes silent and we directly experience Life as it is, as vibrant, alive, radiant Beauty.

Totally Available For Life

Through the years, I have been amazed at how many well intentioned spiritual paths lead individuals to being actually more egocentric, instead of becoming egoless. We may unfortunately find one day that our beautiful, spiritual experiences and glimpses of freedom are meaningless, if we notice that we continue to be self absorbed and arrogant. Our freedom doesn't amount to anything if we just walk around in our own temporary private world of bliss. The important question is *how will we respond to life; how will we act in the world, what kind of person will we be?* What if the sages of the past simply stayed in their caves with their cherished experience of bliss and didn't share their realizations with the world? Would they be any different than a child holding onto a toy? Fortunately for us, they did share—and not in some proselytizing way; they shared themselves from the openness of their hearts. They made themselves *totally available for Life*.

We must realize that the spiritual life is not really about *us* or rather, our ego. Would it make any sense, if it was all about us and our own private experience of peace and bliss? If we ever meet anyone who is far along the path, they know clearly that the path is not about our egoic self. It is about Life living through us; it is about Life waking up to Itself in us, as Us. And when this begins to happen, it is quite a different experience, than the experience of our small self enjoying some spiritual experience.

When we finally realize the depth and surrender that it takes to give this fully, it is too late for our egoic identity. We realize that our life is no longer owned by us and that it never was. We have *always* belonged to the Divine. Our limited egoic identity may think otherwise; but at some point we have to be willing to give up our attachment to our egoic identity, which paradoxically can only happen through Grace. At some point we are given a choice: we can cooperate with Grace or resist it. So the question is: are we willing to let go into our own Divinity? Are we willing to let go and get out of the way and become the very movement of Life Itself?

The Wheel of Samsara

Most of us start off the spiritual path thinking that freedom means we get what we want, when we want it. From the perspective of our ego, this is freedom. We have all had the experience of trying to find happiness by attempting to get everything we want. One of the basic programs of our ego could be summed up with something like, *give me what I want and then I will be happy* (or at least *I* will stop being so obnoxious). This sounds a lot like a 5 year-old and we find somewhere along the way that even when we get what we want, we really aren't that happy, at least not for long. So we try chasing something else. This is what is referred to as *samsara* in the East—the never ending chasing after egoic hopes and dreams, and running from our fears.

If we have been through life long enough, we realize chasing after *this* or *that* does not bring lasting happiness. The funny thing is, most of us still continue to chase the insatiable desires of our mind, even though we know that when we get what we desire, we still will not fully be content. To make discovering this truth more difficult, the human mind has a *forgetting* program running in it. Shortly after we get what we want, a new desire arises and we forget the past promise of happiness that our ego previously tempted us with and we start on a new search for happiness in the next temping dream that comes forward and this keeps us running in circles. Our mind promises us that happiness is just right around the corner, yet once we get around the corner another desire comes forward with the same message. The Buddhists refer to this as the *wheel of samsara*. It goes round and round, like a merry-go-round. Most of us never realize this and remain living trapped in samsara, never realizing that we can hop off at any moment.

But eventually, if we are wise, or if our experience becomes too painful, we hop off, and this is often referred to as Awakening. When we see *through* the nature of our mind—we wake up out of it and we see clearly that our mind is simply a series of programs. As long as we believe in the contents of our minds or the movements of these psychological forces, we will be asleep in samsara. If we can step out of our mind, not from some cold mental or analytical place—but from a deeper place than mind, we can be free. If we can step back into Awareness as who and what we are, and see our mind for what it is, we can experience freedom and clarity. This perspective will solidify as we continually choose to step out of samsara and into Reality.

A common mistake for us is to step out of one egoic way of seeing and into another. Some seekers mistakenly step into their analytical minds and call this an awakening. They begin to analyze themselves and others from some cold scientific place, but this is absolutely not what I am speaking about. Analyzing is simply another movement of mind within the mind. When we are stuck in our minds or we are on autopilot our life will not *feel* alive and vibrant; it will feel cold, mental or numb. One of the big indicators of a true awakening is how rich and intimate our experience of life is. If we are lacking richness and intimacy in life, often it is because we are still stuck in our mentality. When we step into the vast perspective of awareness, there is an overwhelming feeling of tremendous relief—a spacious unity and our experience feels incredibly alive. This shift in consciousness is quite different then the experience of egoic consciousness, which feels cold and numb and is experienced as being divisive, stressful, limiting, and inherently separate. Most individuals do not even know how painfully separate egoic consciousness is because they have never consciously left it. When we eventually wake up out of our mentality, it is a radically different life.

Most humans know fully what it is like on the wheel of samsara. We chase something and then it eventually doesn't work or we get bored of it and then we chase something else, until we realize that we are in fact, going nowhere. Many of us have had the experience of witnessing a moment of clarity and have noticed that this clarity only lasts until we get bored and allow ourselves to be fooled again by our minds. It takes great courage to step off the wheel and stay off it. This experience of stepping out of the past can be a very liberating, or confusing or even frightening moment for most of us. We all know how to live from the mind, but at some point our experience becomes too painful and we begin to ask, if there is another way to live? At some point we may turn to spirituality and begin to ask ourselves questions that lead us beyond our mental way of being. We may begin to hear about freedom and awakening and ask ourselves *what does it mean to live from Freedom or the Awakened state?* As we explore these questions, we are invited out of our old habitual way of being and into the something unknown. For most of us, as we step into the unknown and give up the safety of what we know, we are asked to live in a way that fully includes feeling and experiencing life. Most of us think we know the world of feeling, but as long as we are stuck in our heads, we really don't experience a life of incredible intimacy. If we are going to walk into the world of freedom and unity, we must be willing to be *overwhelmed by intimacy* with life, because this is one of the ways oneness is experienced.

The great Zen Master Dogen described Enlightenment as "intimacy with all things." I love this explanation the most, because it brings forth the direct experience or *feeling* of awakening. But awakening is more than a feeling or an experience—both feelings and experiences come and go; awakening is that which sees the comings and goings of Life. Essentially, awakening is a *shift* in perspective, a shift out of the lens of the mind and into directly experiencing life as it is. This is a common confusion among seekers, because most of the world only experiences life through the lens or projection of mind. So enlightenment is often mistakenly, lumped into the category of another experience or the "ultimate experience." But all projections or feelings and experiences come and go. Awakening, on the other hand, is not simply a passing feeling or an experience or a projection of the mind. Awakening or Enlightenment must be greater than things that come and go— otherwise it would just be another passing *experience*. Similarly, freedom simply could not be just a feeling. If freedom was just a feeling, how powerful would it be when our feeling is gone or challenged? Awakening or freedom is outside or beyond the world of *experience* and *feeling*; and it is paradoxically tangibly experienced in our humanity. Awakening is also beyond having a broad mental or objective perspective. It is beyond all perspectives. As my teacher once said to me, "have no perspective." To get a sense of this, one must step out of the limited viewpoint of oneself. When we step out of this, the self-imposed barriers of the mind collapse, and the direct experience of this is a wonderful and beautiful intimacy with all things, with Life itself. We experience intimacy, because we are not choosing to put mind and thought, which is essentially divisive, between us and the world. This is often experienced viscerally as oneness. Intimacy is the direct visceral experience of oneness.

Another common confusion is that awakening is some mental perspective or some great intellectual understanding. Again this is absolutely not the case. Awakening is not a mental understanding about the nature of Life. It is a direct experience of oneness and of being Life Itself at the same time. This direct experience extends to all levels of our being, because the dividing line between our ego, and the different parts of our being, and the rest of life, falls away. This is realized everywhere at once in us and all around us, because we become one with Life, which is ground shaking to our being on all levels, and simultaneously humbling to our egoic sense of self. In a sense, the very realization destroys who and what we think we are and leaves us vast and intimate with all of life. Paradoxically, this vastness and oneness is so inclusive that it even includes our very egoic self.

It is common for many individuals on the path to get a *glimpse* of this intimacy and hugeness of perspective at various moments of their life; yet a glimpse is quite different than an actual *shift* in perspective. A shift in perspective is permanent. A glimpse comes and goes. When we get a glimpse and are still plugged into our ego, then we will have an *experience* of awakening that comes and eventually goes. As this experience leaves our field we will then feel compelled to chase the *experience* of awakening with our ego, which is quite different than an actual shift in perspective *out of ego*. Another common egoic tendency is to want to continue to experience this *feeling* of awakening and to try to hold onto it or to try to possess it. Often as we do this, the experience of intimacy is lost by choosing to believe in grasping and uniting again in the normal human perspective, which is a dualistic perspective toward all of life. In a sense, the quickest way out of the world of awakening is to believe our own thoughts or the movements of our egoic psychological forces. As soon as we do, we again believe in the perspective of *me* and *you*, of *this* and *that*; which is radically different than being or living from a place of nondivision or oneness. To clarify, nondivision is the nonperspective of enlightenment, where all is One. It is experienced as life without a center or life beyond ego, which is freedom. Duality is the normal human condition where we believe the thoughts in our mind, and identify with them, which creates an *us* and a *them*; it creates a *me* and duality and separation. Neither way of being is good or bad; they are simply two entirely different ways of being in the world. One way of being is living as Unity, and the other way of being believes in the identity of us as ego and creates division in our world. We can look at our nightly news and see what our dualistic way of living has created, and we can imagine how different a nondualistic relationship to life would be like. The choice is ours in every moment.

For thousands of years, awakening has been such a mysterious thing, only experienced by those living in caves or monasteries, but it can be quite simple actually, and accessible to any of us. In a sense, it requires the courage to not believe what we think and to be willing to directly experience Life as it is, without the projection of the lens of our past. Furthermore, to continue to stay awake, it is helpful to be able to discern what is True, so that we do not become tricked by our minds again. When we start believing in our own nonsense, we take a perspective as *this person* or *that person* and give up our Freedom which is beyond identification with a personal egoic self. When we lose the awakened perspective, what actually happens is that we *choose* to align with our thoughts, instead of choosing to be intimate with the direct experience of Life as it is in every moment.

Another common confusion or myth about awakening is that our minds must be empty of thought to be free. It would be incorrect to say that if there are thoughts, there is no Freedom. More correctly, if we believe the foolishness or the seductive nature of our thinking, then there is no Freedom. Thoughts, thinking, feelings, and pain all can be present, and all are welcome in the spacious nature of Freedom. Too many spiritual seekers falsely believe that one must stop all thoughts and be pain free in order to be Free, but the mind and our feeling nature doesn't stop after Awakening. It is just that we stop *believing* in the movement of the mind, as what's real (including our thoughts about pain) and we stop *identifying* 100% with the contents of our minds.

What we begin to rest in is beyond words, beyond feeling, beyond points of views and intimate with all of Life, as Life Itself—as the vastness that includes and embraces everything without exception.

What is beyond the transcendent?

For one to become fully liberated one must walk through three main stages of enlightenment. The first is the *transcendental awakening*, which is the most common type of spiritual awakening. This awakening is an awakening out of our mentality and into the transcendental space above. The next major awakening that follows is the *awakening of our heart*, where we experience an incredible intimacy and unity with all of life. Beyond this is an awakening that happens deep in our gut, where we wake up to our *fearless indestructibility*. This final awakening is often experienced or felt like a mountain of emptiness within. This awakening is usually what is referred to as our final liberation. But ultimately, as long as we have a human form there are countless layers and levels of awakening, transformation, and embodiment. In this following chapter, I would like to focus on what is beyond the initial transcendent awakening.

After the huge opening of a transcendental awakening, the explosion of our consciousness out of and beyond the body, mind, and emotional centers, there is a homecoming of our consciousness back into our humanity. Initial awakenings tend to be marked by an ecstatic, yet naïve period filled with astounding grace and blissful spaciousness, and are experienced as overwhelmingly heavenly and transcendent in their nature. They literally shake us out of our being, and we experience boundless freedom. We may experience this overwhelming bliss and cosmic consciousness for a moment or for years; it is not really up to us. However, at some point a natural integration takes places and ironically we become accustomed to this wonderful new way of being, even though at first it is unimaginable to us that anyone could become accustomed to living in such a vast transcendent Reality. Often as we integrate this initial awakening, there comes such a feeling of totality and completeness that we cannot even imagine how life or our experience could not have *always* included this radical new perspective. Anyone who has this type of awakening will feel amazingly complete and total for *some time*.

But at some point, one of our teachers (who is more experienced and mature) may come along and say that *this is not the end of the path, but the beginning*, and the individual experiencing the transcendent reality will most likely have a very difficult time agreeing. To the one experiencing a transcendent awakening, a feeling of "how dare you," might arise because the completeness of their current state is felt to be so amazingly total that it is extremely hard for them to believe that there could be more to life than this. But anyone who has made it beyond the initial stages of awakening will gently smile because there is always more. Maturity shows us this, and this type of maturity comes from the experience of living beyond the transcendent.

After some time, a day, a month, a few years in my case, we become accustomed to the hugeness, and somewhere along the way, Life begins to point out all the areas where we are still not free. It can be really painful and humiliating to realize, *I am That, I am one with Life, and wow, I still have so much work to do.* On earth, we are humbled by our own humanity again and again. We realize that we are not the next Buddha or Messiah and that we had better be open to doing some more work. But because we have realized the transcendent and know deep in our hearts who we *are*, the work becomes much easier. The work becomes more like getting out of the way and allowing ourselves to be purified and transformed, than something that we are actively *doing* with our egoic wills. If there is any doing, it is actively being open and surrendering all the parts of ourselves that still need work, and there will be plenty of this, despite what our transcendent experience shows us. It is good to be humble and open to growth in the beginning, the middle, and forever. In fact, if we ever feel as if we are done, that we are fully liberated, especially after an initial awakening, we should view this as a big red flag. We may *feel* done, but time and experience will show us otherwise.

After we spend some time in the transcendent realm, our consciousness tends to energetically descend back down into our bodies. When we are in the transcendent, we feel as if we are as big as the sky, our consciousness feels vast and free, and no thoughts seem to stick in this vast perspective. In an unhealthy way, we may become out of touch with our lives and relationships. It may be almost impossible to avoid this, because our new perspective *feels* so overwhelmingly huge that *dealing* in a normal practical human way seems, at times, like a great *inconvenience*. Yet here is the first sign that our awakening could be more inclusive and is not total. Other common signs of this arrogance are seen when our ego comes forward and begins to claim the identity of the awakened one, and we begin to act superior or like a know it all. This too almost always happens, in the beginning of an initial awakening. Fortunately, Life will not let us get away with this and will show us exactly where we are not awake—where we still have pride or arrogance or are living in delusion. As we align with these egoic aspects of our unconsciousness our vast experience will begin to fade and as this happens, there is a coming home into our humanity and we will discover that we have more work to do. However, if our awakening is a true shift in perspective and not simply another "spiritual experience," we will bring with us our transcendent perspective. Because of this vast vision that we now have, working with our humanity can be quite simple, because in a sense we are free of ourselves, yet paradoxically still fully human. We still laugh, cry and experience pain, but it all happens In thIs tremendous space of freedom. Many of us wish that we could just wake up, be fully liberated, complete, and pain free, and then go home. But this world is an evolutionary world, and there is no end to evolution. It is true that our unborn nature is already, always brilliant and complete, but our humanity is ever evolving. After spending time with a teacher, our children, our partner or our friends, we will humbly see that we need to continue to work on our humanity and that we are not perfected Buddhas, living with complete compassion in every moment.

For thousands of years, enlightenment has been shrouded in myth and in secret teachings, which has lead to so much confusion about its nature. There are many spiritual myths which lead us to believe that if we wake up, we become perfect. Within these myths, are many unconscious ideas that awakening is somehow equated with some ideal state of perfection, but the whole idea of us becoming "perfect" needs to be examined. Where does this idea come from, and who are we to put such pressure on ourselves or our teachers, to be perfect, we may ask? No one, if you spend an extended amount of time with, will ever live up to our *ideas* of perfection. A better attitude may be to continually examine ourselves for places where we are still acting from an egoic or limited perspective and to always be open to continued feedback from the various teachers that Life provides. If we are honest, we will notice that we can continually learn no matter where we are on the path, and we can humbly see that our outward expression of Truth can always be improved upon. In fact, after we wake up, our path becomes about *closing the gap* between what we have realized and how we live in the world. In the beginning the gap can be quite large. If we are honest, we find that our outward expression of our deepest realizations will always be playing catch up with the innate perfection of our inner radiance, yet the more closely the two become aligned, the clearer and less dramatic our life will become.

With an attitude of beginner's mind or complete openness, we will be more apt to experience freedom in relationship to our own humanity and to others. If we try to compare our transcendent realization to the experience of our human life, we will see that we just don't measure up. Beginner's mind is just as helpful in the beginning as it is after we awaken. Having a beginner's mind is especially useful, as we come back from our initial period of heavenly transcendence and back into our humanity and embrace our ordinary human lives. It is incredibly painful as we go from the perspective of boundless transcendent freedom, to descending back into a conditioned body, mind, and emotions. In my own experience, I was completely enthralled by my initial transcendent awakening. In the beginning of my initial awakening, I went back and forth between being awake to being lost within the confines of my mind. At some point, this transcendent awakening stabilized, and I thought *I finally made it*; for months I lived in an overwhelming and constant state of bliss and peace. Then to my utter dismay, I began to notice my ego coming forward again; I saw various places in my life where I was still reacting to life in ugly and unconscious ways. As this continued to happen again and again, I tried to simply transcend my ego, but my unconsciousness kept showing up in my daily life. At some point I realized that I could not transcend all of my life; I realized that I was not growing, but simply transcending or trying to transcend the inconvenient aspects of my life. Arrogantly I felt that I could simply rise above it all, but at some point I saw that I could not rise above every aspect of my humanity. As I saw this fully, the energy and transcendent perspective of my awakening descended energetically down into my body and ego and I was shocked by the pain of limitation again. This stage is a necessary process of our complete awakening, because without again descending back into our egoic conditioning, we will not be able to transform our ego. If we stay in the transcendent reality, our ego will remain untouched and still be able to cause trouble for us and others.

This process of reentering our humanity is such a confusing time, because we are illuminated by the transcendent light of awareness, yet find ourselves tripping over our ego in countless ways. However, this is actually a beautiful humbling experience and it gives us the opportunity to *transform* ourselves which is radically more powerful than *transcending* ourselves. When we transcend, our perspective changes but perhaps our habitual actions do not always change. Yet we transform when, we go to the root of our identity through the process of embracing our humanity with love. As we do this work, we begin to deeply change and transmute on countless levels, and eventually, this transmutation will be the very ground that we stand on.

Too often, this transformational stage of awakening is not even mentioned, because it is falsely assumed that awakening is some total and complete transition that happens all at once. Yet this is not the case in reality. If this homecoming back into our humanity is in any way resisted, the pain of this descent of consciousness will increase. Yet, if this process is seen as a normal and necessary stage, then compassion for our conditioned nature will arise. This compassion is what is needed for a deeper purification and transformation to take place. Attitudes of compassion, acceptance, humility, and beginner's mind will be our best friends in this process. If we do not understand the necessity and importance of this evolutionary process of consciousness descending from the transcendent back into our humanity, we may find ourselves resisting it, thinking we did something wrong, or deeply confused by what is happening. Yet this is again, wonderful opportunity, because we are literally transforming all the places within us that we are still lost in the confusion and delusion of our egos. It would be impossible to come into this stage of transformation, without losing our minds. In fact losing our minds is the whole point. While we let go and allow our minds to be lost, the various places within us that are letting go will scream, shout and resist their death and dissolution into spaciousness. For some time our clear, silent awakening will be filled with cries and tears of letting go as we walk deeper into what it means to be free.

Although the initial experience of our transcendent awakening seems to come suddenly and blast our consciousness out of our bodies, a deeper awakening happens within us that often looks more like a process than a sudden shift. This process can take anywhere from a few years to a lifetime, depending how open and willing we are to give way to it or how deep God chooses to take us. As this process begins, we find ourselves face to face again, with our own humanity, the very thing we were excited to get away from. But we are reminded by the great teachers, that freedom is not about getting away from anything, freedom includes everything, and even every part of our being without exception. My teacher has often reminded me that God builds upon us, and although at times, it can feel like a destructive process, in the end it is a process of evolution in embodiment and deepening in Love, not of death and destruction, although it may feel this way to our ego and sense of self.

So as we descend back into our bodies, there may be huge parts of ourselves that resist this movement to include our humanity. There will be feelings of contraction, as we go from cosmic to gross states of consciousness, and there may be feelings of pain, irritation, and very much ordinariness. But if one begins to look closely, we see that this hugeness is still quite here. The Silence is still here, and we may still have a busy, conditioned mind, but now we have a choice. This choice is essential, for our freedom lies in our ability to choose the huge, vast Silence as our identity and where we *respond* to life from. If instead, we choose to be the nonsense of our minds, we will again delude ourselves and walk back into the prison that we were so happy to have left. But now that we have tasted freedom, we will not be able to stay in the jailhouse of our mind too long; it will simply be too painful.

As the ordinariness of our humanity comes forward again in our consciousness, it may seem like a huge letdown in comparison to the transcendent awakening we were once living in. But the more we sit with this, the more we realize that *both are here*. We may not be walking around totally blissed out all the time, but there will still be a huge spaciousness and silence that is grounded in this world. And from this groundedness, we begin to be useful to the Divine. She will begin to embody us and use us for Her work. We will begin to become an instrument for the Divine. We will quickly realize that awakening has nothing to do with us *feeling better* or escaping this world. It has to do with surrendering to God so that God's plan, God's agenda can manifest in Reality. It is humbling to realize that, as my teacher said, "We wake up to be God's slave. But in this slavery is our freedom." The more we get out of the way and let Her move us, the more free we become. At some point, as Her will and ours become one, we experience a freedom so deep that there are no words for it.

Yet no matter where we are on the path, it is necessary to remember to start where you are and the work tends to be the same; no matter where you begin, it is about letting go and surrendering to the Divine. To be free in this world, we continue to work on all the rough parts of our mind and emotional bodies. We may seek out the help of teachers or counselors to help clean up our outward expression of our inner divinity. We may do shadow work, so that we don't continue to trip over our shadow again and again, causing pain for ourselves and others. We again dive down into the dark, painful and twisted parts of our psyche and begin to unearth our unconsciousness. To fully see clearly here, we often need a guide to point out the places within us that are still hidden from our brilliance. To be awake does not mean that we don't still have blind spots, conditioning, or egoic tendencies. Often with awakening, much of this is quickly dissolved or is seen through from the perspective of the transcendent. But a shocking realization comes after we return from our honeymoon, and we see that much of our past is still haunting us in the present. Countless individuals have had wonderful awakenings on retreat and upon coming home found themselves irritated by their partners or children for "disturbing the peace." It is not that the insight they found on retreat was not true, but coming home is a reminder that we have more work to do. We can remember that there are always more layers and levels to our growth, to awakening. I don't think that I can overemphasize this point: No matter how deep our realization, we have more work to do, perhaps forever. When we realize this, we give up the need for any absolute end or completion to our humanity and instead we happily grow into our ever greater expression of the Love that we are.

Letting go of the Protective Stance of Ego

Our ego's primary function is to protect ourselves from real or perceived pain. One of the ways it does this is through creating an energetic and psychosomatic wall or armor around and within us. This subconscious movement protects us against mental, emotional and physical pain by creating a boundary between us and the pain within us or the experience of a new or expected pain. This movement to protect ourselves tends to come forward at a moment of a real or perceived crisis. In these situations our bodies, minds and emotions instinctively go tense in an effort to brace ourselves from being overwhelmed by feelings. To protect ourselves from being overwhelmed, our egos put a wall around our heart or other aspects of ourselves so that we are not harmed by the unpredictable forces of our emotions or the emotions or behaviors of another. Sometimes the ego remains stuck in this moment of fear and continues to hold up a wall against what has come and perhaps, now left or what never actually came into our physical reality.

As therapist and teacher, I have worked with many individuals throughout the years that have carried heavy layers of egoic armoring in their bodies, often years after the original painful experience occurred. These layers of armor contain cellular memories that are stored, sometimes for decades, after an experience of pain or trauma originally took place. I learned how to work with healing and releasing these walls, from years of working with my teachers and healing and releasing my own layers of armoring and cellular memories. To this day, I continue to work with liberating myself from years of holding my body tight and tense in an effort to shield myself from being hurt by often, imagined fears.

Of course there are times when these fears are real and are actively arising in the present moment. If this is the case, it is wise to take action first, get ourselves to a safe place, and do whatever we need to do to take care of ourselves before we begin to participate in the deep work of healing and releasing trauma or cellular memories of the past. Our emotional body will not open up and heal, if we are still in an unsafe situation, which is why it is fully appropriate for us to do this work in a safe and supportive environment.

What I find amazing about this unconscious armoring that takes place within us, is that when we experience pain or overwhelming feelings of the past, we may continue to unconsciously hold our egoic shields up for years after we experienced the original overwhelming feeling. We often hold ourselves tense to protect ourselves from a person who is no longer in our lives or who we might only see 1% of the time. We may have had a harsh mother or father and as a child, we put up walls to protect ourselves from their harshness, but still have not put these walls down. At the time it was a developmentally appropriate thing for us to do, but years later how many of us still hold egoic walls to protect us, from parents who may no longer be alive or are not present in our lives? Maybe we will never see the person who originally hurt us again, and yet unconsciously we still armor ourselves against a "one day," chance encounter. We may continue to hold this protection simply out of habit, even though there is no longer a threat. What is ironic is that the act of holding or bracing ourselves, does not ever really protect us in any practical way, yet our ego tries to put up any walls it can to "defend" itself against pain. In a sad way it is trying its hardest to somehow save us from feeling, which is actually unavoidable.

It may be that be that our body was once shocked by a sudden accident or trauma and as a result a trauma response began. Because of this, we began to habitually brace ourselves against the unexpected, yet never realized that we could let our guard down and we continued to hold ourselves tense for years. Whatever the case, this unconscious psychosomatic phenomena can cut us off from fully experiencing the rawness, the beauty and wonder of Life. To be awake means that we open and include all of our being in our experience of life. But if there are parts of ourselves that are unconsciously resisting or armoring ourselves from life, it will be difficult to experience beauty and spaciousness in these parts of ourselves. After we discover the places within ourselves where we are unconsciously holding tension, we can invite our body to open and relax there. But again for our body to relax, we must first be in a safe environment and feel emotionally and mentally safe. This might mean a change of relationship, or environment, or simply realizing that we are perfectly safe right here, right now, as we begin to differentiate between this moment and the past.

After we have slowed down and taken the time to establish a feeling of safety in ourselves, we can talk in a gentle way to our bodies or the various parts of ourselves that are in pain, that are still holding up walls and let them know that *we are loved* and *it is safe to relax. It is safe to put the shield down, it is safe to let go. We no longer have to hold this tension in our bodies*. If we speak in a way that our body can hear, then it will listen to us and begin to relax. Although, if we speak to ourselves in harsh or judgmental ways, we will not feel safe and we might become more scared and more tense. I like to think of talking to the places within us that are still hurting, like a good parent would talk to a child. We can use a soft and reassuring voice, a voice that is calm and clear; when we talk in this way, it becomes easy for our pain to hear us and our body may start to relax in a very gentle and natural way. Although if we have been through deep trauma and pain, much more work will be necessary and we may find ourselves trembling, or deeply grieving—but this is good. We should not be scared; this is the process of letting go. We let go when we embrace everything with an open heart. As this pain arises, I usually like to say the phrases *you are safe, you are loved,* over and over again to the place of pain in my body for however long it takes—a minute or a month.

Usually trauma is stored on top of our heart (in our chest area), in our throat, our solar plexus, deep in our belly or pelvis. To heal, I get quiet, lay down and open to the hugeness of the Divine Mother or my True Nature. I place one hand on my heart and the other on the pain and fully bring my awareness to the place of pain within me. I begin to say these phrases over and over again, usually for one to fifteen minutes and typically begin to feel the pain begin to open, release and heal as I lie in meditation holding a space for letting go. The process of letting go tends to be experienced as a trembling in the body, along with a feeling of energy moving, often releasing tears, pain and even laughter. Sometimes memories begin to unravel and release and as they do, I simply allow them to pass by, loving and acknowledging them, yet not getting absorbed with the memories in a mental way. I stay with the *felt* experience of pain releasing and continue offering the loving words to myself. Sometimes, if I feel separate from or outside of my pain, I imagine my pain is a raging river and I visualize myself jumping into the river and allow myself to fully cry or laugh or get angry and allow whatever feeling that is here to fully move through my body, without getting involved in any of the thoughts or stories that go along with the pain. When we get preoccupied with the thoughts or stories of our pain, we actually go into our minds and create a distance from our pain. To fully release our pain and allow our walls of ego to dissolve, we must join and *feel* the pain fully.

After my divorce, I can remember the intense pain that I experienced and held in my body. I sat intentionally with this pain each day and everyday for over a year, using a very specific meditation practice for helping to release this pain. I sat down and relaxed my body; I took deep breaths and became open and spacious inside. From this quiet, open and spacious place, I would locate the pain in my body, often this was quite easy to find. The wonderful thing about pain is that it is uncomfortable, loud and undeniable. The practice was to fully sit with the pain and fully allow it to be here. If we do not *fully allow it to be,* we will simply not heal. When we first embrace our pain, our minds habitually turn and run in the opposite direction. They often do this by thinking of something very important that needs to be done right now. Or it fantasizes about some other place or person or it starts planning the day. The mind will try to do anything but sit with pain. It can be humorous to watch how quickly our minds go somewhere else when pain is in the room. It can find something else to do in a fraction of a second. Our minds will avoid pain at all costs, so it is quite a task just to get ourselves to sit with pain and allow ourselves to fully acknowledge it. Yet to heal, we must love ourselves enough to take the time to make healing our priority.

After we have opened and allowed the pain to be here fully, we might imagine that the pain is a child and it is sitting in our lap. As a father, I love this image. I simply think of my daughter and remember that any time she fell and was hurt, the first thing I wanted to do was to pick her up and hold her. We must cultivate this type of love for ourselves and the pain that lives within us. We have to *want* to hold it. Although most of us, want to get rid of this pain as soon as we feel it. But if we want to get rid of it, we miss our chance to be free. We miss our chance to know love. We miss our chance to transform pain into Peace.

For this process to be truly healing, we have to be totally open and to *want* to sit with it. Another image that I like comes from the ancient Zen teachings on the angry bull. If we have an angry bull, and want it to calm down, then we let it run around in a big open field. We work with pain in the same way; as we open to the pain and allow it to fully be within us, it may even become louder, it may need to run around for awhile. What is helpful, is for us to notice all the space in our mind and our bodies, in our awareness and to notice that this space has no end. From this spacious openness, we can allow the pain to spread out and unravel in our spacious awareness. This invitation also, helps our ego to relax and begin to know that there is plenty of space for all this pain to move around in, and that we no longer have to contain or hold this energy within ourselves. As we open to our already spacious nature, which is always here, we may notice that our pain might make a fuss; it might send awful memories through our minds. To fully let go and heal, these memories must be seen, heard and acknowledged—but not indulged. By this I mean, that we see in the present moment that it (the experience that is feared) is not actually happening any longer, that it happened in the past and now that it is the *present* and we are safe, and that we do not need to continue thinking and repeating these thoughts and stories anymore.

If we continue to indulge in the stories and thoughts, then we get stuck in the past and the mind is again successful in distracting us from sitting fully with the pain and so, we do not heal. Sometimes, we need to allow for these thoughts to go on and on until they wear themselves out. But it becomes very dangerous, when we believe in our stories and add to them in the present. If we do this, we will continue the story and never free the pain from ourselves until, we go back and fully allow it to release through the process of fully acknowledging and feeling our pain.

If we can be this open and this willing, the pain will release in a very powerful way when it's ready, and this is up to it, not us; the only thing we can do is fully accept what's here and surrender. This is a very important point. The pain must feel safe and fully accepted and not denied in any way and then it will release. As it releases, we may experience a wonderful power or energy running through our body, or a terrifying energy or emotion. Most people when they experience this terror or overwhelming sensations for the first few times, become scared and quit this work by leaving their felt experience and going back to their mind or distract themselves in one form or another in an effort to avoid fully facing and embracing what is within us. When we stop the process, it is as if a wonderful energetic release was beginning, and we instead gave up and ran back to the comfort of our habitual minds and thoughts, and as a result remain stuck in the mud, only to have to come back and face it again one day.

If this happens, (and it almost always does in the beginning) we don't have to be discouraged—there will be another chance. When we are willing to again open to the pain, sit with it fully and allow for it to release, we will experience a wonderful and terrible feeling of being out of control. Our invitation is to allow ourselves to experience this fully— to fully embrace feeling *out of control*. This is what it feels like to let go of deeply held emotions and be free; it will feel as if uncontrollable sensations are moving through our body. Just like when we are deeply emotional, it feels uncontrollable, but this experience of letting go into an uncontrollable release of energy is very much normal and OK. It might be the scariest experience of our life; we may turn red or pale, and feel sick to our stomachs. But this is all a part of the process of consciously letting go. It can be helpful to lie down in bed, and allow ourselves to be fully supported by the bed and breathe deeply into our belly. As we allow ourselves to let go, to turn pale, and to be terrified, we breathe; we realize that we are OK and in the end, we realize that we will not die from this experience of letting go, although our minds may scream and shout and *act* like we are walking straight into death. As we fully allow the emotions and overwhelming sensations to fully be here, these very emotions will turn to pure energy and a rush of energy will begin to run out of our body. This movement may last for a second, a minute, an hour, a day or longer. But when we open to the movement of emotions and see that it is just energy and do not believe the thoughts that say *we are going to die;* we become free. This is what it viscerally feels like to consciously let go of deeply held trauma or cellular memories while allowing the walls of ego to collapse. We see that it is just energy running through our body and we allow for it to move in whatever way it needs. Depending on the depth of the pain, it may take just one meditation on the pain or a hundred meditations to heal what is within us. If we become comfortable with working with ourselves in this way, this fearlessness will become a way of life and we will come to love going into the unconscious parts of ourselves that are hurting. We will find that the majority of the pain we experience is nothing more than energy stuck in our body from the past. With the realization that pain is energy and the willingness to embrace any of it, we become fearlessly free.

Why do I have so many voices in my head?

Within minutes of sitting down to meditate, many of us begin wondering why there are so many different or conflicting voices in our minds. This inner chaos and conflict is why so many of us avoid being, quiet or alone. We may notice that when we are silent, a mix of unresolved personal issues, arguments, hopes, dreams and desires, come forward asking for our attention. Most of us in the digital age have a need to be constantly plugged in or online, not necessarily because there is some information we actually need, but because we use electronics as a way of avoiding or distracting ourselves from the chaos of our own minds. These chaotic and conflicting voices are why we and our world are so insane. Almost everyone struggles with this insanity for the extent of their lives and accept it as a normal aspect of being human. Yet for those of us, who in a rare moment, have heard the deep voice of the heart and have experienced the clarity that comes with it, we may begin to wonder why we can't live from this place of clarity always and instead find ourselves lost most of the time in the crazy world of our minds. There is a very logical explanation why we are so conflicted inside; it is because we have three major egoic minds within us: a mental mind, an emotional mind and a physical mind. These three minds cloud and cover the simple and clear voice of our intuitive Heart, which is an entirely different type of consciousness within us than our minds. The nature of our Heart essence is Divinity, whereas the nature of our mind is based in a habitual reaction of hopes, fears and survival. With this mix of egoic minds and Divinity within us, it can be quite confusing to be human.

Most of us struggle greatly with our relationship to these various minds within us and live in a constant state of inner division. This is very much why the human experience is so difficult. Other animals do not struggle with the complexity of mind that we do. A dog's mind is not divided inside, their minds are simple and do not give them much trouble. This is why they are such great friends, and why when we are in their company, we relax in their simplicity. Taking our dogs on a walk can be a joyous experience for us, if we join them in the simplicity of simply walking, feeling the breeze and enjoying nature. If we can let go of our complexity, we too will feel wonderful. Yet if we go on the same walk with them and are busy worrying about our taxes, or having an imaginary argument with our spouse or our boss, or dreaming of getting a new car, we will suffer. For many of us, even practicing meditation does not lead to a feeling of joy or simplicity, when we simply use that time to give audience to all the conflicting voices within. The primary reason most people quit meditating is because they do not want to sit and listen to all these inner voices any longer. Having a complex mind comes with a great difficulty, if we do not know how to work with it.

Many of us have the experience of our mind being painfully divided, which is quite opposite of our true nature. Our true nature is complete, total and absolutely undivided and as we rest in our undivided nature, we experience oneness and unity consciousness. Before we discover our true nature, and embody this clarity and wonderful peace that we are, these three minds within us all fight for our attention and create a sense of chaos within us while they cloud the clarity of our hearts. In the spiritual world this is often referred to as being *lost in the dream of our mind or Maya or samsara*. This experience of being confused and divided is sadly "normal" for the collective consciousness that we live in. Ironically, one of the key criteria when diagnosing someone with a major mental health disorder is if they listen to and believe the "voices" in their minds—something everyone one does to a greater or lesser degree!

Because most of us are lost in this normal experience of subtle insanity, we ignore or are unable to discern the wisdom of our hearts and instead, spend the extent of our lives negotiating with all of our egoic minds, trying to satisfy them so that we experience the least amount of pain and greatest amount of pleasure. We do this because the three voices of our minds are so loud and demanding of our attention, and we have within us an unexamined belief that *if we appease our mind it will be quiet and we will then experience peace*, yet this belief never seems to deliver. For most of the world, our first priority is to appease our egos and then occasionally, we listen to our hearts. We all know this experience of deeply knowing in our hearts which direction we should head and then instead choose to do otherwise, because our egoic minds are so loud and persistent. Perhaps our heart tells us that we don't need to go on a date with Mr. Wrong, but we do because he is handsome and our desire mind convinces us that he is capable of loving us. Or perhaps we know our body does not need any sugar, but we feel lonely and sad so we eat a whole bowl of ice cream. When we listen to the wrong voice, we may experience a temporary relief from pain or experience temporary happiness, but ultimately we suffer. Yet we have a choice whether we live in a temporary fleeting happiness or a long term happiness that comes from knowing how to listen to our heart. When we choose our heart, we end our suffering by acting in alignment with our truth, which brings us the experience of clarity, sanity and lasting happiness. As we continue to live from the depths of our hearts, we will come home to our natural clarity and an unshakable contentment.

Often I am asked, "How do I listen to my heart?" Ironically, this is difficult for most of us, because we have been so educated to use our mental and emotional minds as our way of relating to life. The answer to this question is quite simple; our heart is the still quiet voice within. It lacks the volume and emotionality of the emotional mind, it lacks the argumentative nature of our mentality and it lacks the aggressiveness or craving nature of our physical mind. These three egoic minds usually are loud and demanding and repeat the same stories over and over again, and by contrast, our heart is not loud or overly repetitive it is *simple, quiet and clear.* In fact, when our mind is overly repetitive, it is a red flag for us; it often means there is something within us that needs to be healed, not acted on; yet most of us give into the repetitive nature of our minds just to quiet them. When we give into the repetitive nature of our minds and act on our emotions or in accordance with our grand arguments, we continue to suffer and cause suffering for others. Yet when we act in accordance with our hearts, we experience healing, growth, and deep and lasting happiness.

Our heart is not reactive or overly repetitive like our mind is; our heart is gentle and patient, for it knows in the end that it will prevail. Truth always wins; it is simply a matter of time. Our heart is on Divine time and based in an intuitive intelligence, whereas our mind has no patience because its nature is insecure. Our heart is quiet and wise like our grandmother's wisdom. Our heart is rarely loud, unless we are in a life or death situation. Ninety percent of the time, our heart is gentle and simple. If we are wondering which way to go, it may gently say, *this way*, yet with no reasoning, argument or emotion; it often comes with a mysterious silence and completeness. If we have a question, our heart may simply answer *yes* or *no*, without any explanation why because its' wisdom is omniscient and needs no supporting argument. When our mind speaks, it will come with hours of supporting evidence or with a long story or often with emotions wrapped up in it, because its "intelligence" is based in insecurity. Just like someone who is insecure, our mind will say the same argument over and over again, almost like it has to convince itself of its validity. Our heart may only say what it has to say once, yet when it comes, it does so with a power and a force of truth, that needs no defending. If we are lost in the dividing dance of our mental, emotional and physical minds then our constant invitation is to listen to the quiet voice of our heart and surrender to its wisdom and movement in our lives and watch what beautifully, unfolds.

Most of us struggle to be this simple; most of us choose instead to be very complicated and miss the beauty that comes when we listen to the simple, yet powerful wisdom of our hearts. Learning to be simple is mostly what the spiritual path is about, the more simple we become the easier it is for us to wake up, because we are no longer getting involved in the chaos of our minds. As we choose simplicity as a way of being, we experience such a relief from living outside of this chaos and our lives begin to become filled with such a peace and unity.

After this awakening has deeply matured, we experience an entirely new type of clarity that comes when all of these conflicting voices drop away and we are simply left with one voice; the voice of the Divine within us and we no longer experience competing voices or have to choose which voice to listen to. It becomes so quiet inside, as our inward division begins to dissolve, and eventually, it becomes quite difficult to be inwardly divided any longer. The very fabric of our mind heals its divisive nature as we no longer are living in or moved by fear. Instead, our mind becomes reoriented in the oneness of unity consciousness. As our orientation shifts from an egoic and divided consciousness and into unity consciousness, we discover that our thoughts are not separate from God's thoughts; our mind is not separate from God's mind. When we come to this place, we become one movement, which is experienced as an absolute sanity. This shift is nothing we could ever *do* or *choose*, for the one who wants to *do* this no longer exists. This dissolving of our competing egoic minds is something that we surrender to, not something that we are in charge of healing. This process of dissolving is our doorway into unity consciousness, into our liberation.

But for those of us who do not yet live permanently in unity consciousness, we need to understand our minds so that we can begin to have a sane relationship with these minds and what arises within us. We have no choice but to start where ever we are and begin to examine our various minds, and attempt to bring them into an alignment or some sense of manageable sanity. For those of us who are not awake or those who vacillate back and forth between the egoic and awakened perspective, we may find it helpful to understand the perspective of each of these minds, so that we can understand the workings of the chaos within. Most individuals, when they look inside see a mess of conflicting thoughts and emotions and generally call this mess, *"me."* But there are other times in life, when we have a natural clarity. This is what most of us would like to experience all the time. Yet the majority of the time, we do not experience this clarity, but instead live in the suffering of confusion and division. Before we let go into the vast intelligence of liberation and these egoic voices have dissolved and cease to arise again, it is wise to understand the different minds and their qualities or perspectives, so that we can see clearly while in the midst of the storms of our minds. Even if we are not permanently awake to our true nature, with *mindfulness* we can see that we are not our minds, because we have the ability to reflect upon them. Knowing this changes our whole relationship to the dance of mind within. At any moment we are free to step into the one who simply *sees*, and from this perspective we can begin to examine what is within us and create a clarity of being.

There are many ways we can become clear inside. We naturally experience clarity when all of our minds effortlessly align, but when this does not happen, we can be proactive by using our gift of choice. We can experience clarity if we choose to listen to one mind, and not the others. This type of clarity requires discipline and discernment. When we are conflicted inside and have to choose, the general rule is to *choose* to listen to whichever mind is in alignment with our deepest values or intuition. This may require us to listen to the voice that is *not* the loudest, but quite possibly the softest voice within. The softest, most innocent voice within is the voice of our heart. To listen to our heart, we need to have the ability to stop and listen deeply. This may require discipline if we are not accustomed to slowing down or deeply listening. Our emotional mind may be loud and have all of our attention, but it is often not in alignment with our highest values. Often it is responding from a place of hope, fear or attachment. Sometimes we have to make decisions that can be quite difficult, like leaving someone we love, because they are hurting us. This can be hard because we love them and are afraid to lose them, yet if we are going to honor ourselves, we must listen to the quiet, innocent voice that says *we must move on*. Yet we can *choose* to still stay open and move on from a place of deep love, instead of emotional reactivity. This is the challenge of listening to our Heart. The voice of our heart will lead to greater opening which includes greater feeling, both *good* and *bad* feelings and everything in between. Listening to our heart means we are opening to feeling everything; our heart does not discriminate against feelings, in fact to our heart, it may not matter which direction is difficult or feels uncomfortable, our heart still goes forward.

In contrast, our egoic mind will absolutely, try to seek pleasure and avoid pain, even if this means making short term bad decisions, to avoid pain. When we listen to our emotional minds we are usually trying to grasp at something or push it away from a place of insecurity and anxiety. Whereas, when we respond from the heart, we meet life with openness, courage, and Love—even if what we are meeting is painful. Too often, I have seen individuals who have made the short term bad decision to stay in an abusive relationship, because they were avoiding the pain of leaving the relationship. We can see why listening to our emotional mind, is not often the most helpful voice to listen to. Listening to our heart can be difficult at first, but in the end we will be unimaginably happier that we did.

The 3 egoic minds:

Our entire lives we live plagued by our three minds and inner voices, all struggling with each other creating an insane and confusing inner dialogue that never seems to fully resolve itself. Yet the *full* process of spiritual awakening ends this dance. It does so when the transformative power of awakening has worked its way through the three major minds, and has transformed them into one. It is not until these three major awakenings which happen in the head, heart and gut have fully completed themselves will this inner division be resolved. With most individuals who experience an *initial* awakening, there is a huge sense of relief, from a shift in perspective out of our conflicting minds and into the transcendent reality. But this shift does not necessarily end all inner confusion and insanity, because during initial awakenings we tend to *transcend* ourselves, which is quite different than *transforming* our egoic minds or humanity.

When we transcend something, we often just leave it behind, unchanged—which means it can rise again within us. Yet when something is transformed, it becomes something altogether different. When we transform our anger, we become clear and decisive. When we transform sadness, we become innocent, tender and also strong. Yet if we simply transcend our egoic conditioning, we may feel that it is no longer within us, but given the right circumstances it will rise again. It is not until we have experienced awakening within the head, heart and gut and have spent years of post awakening inner work while maturing in our awakened embodiment does this egoic insanity transform or dissolve into unity.

This process is one of learning to fearlessly love and embrace whatever arises within our consciousness. As our awakening deepens and includes every aspect of ourselves and our lives without exception, our orientation radically shifts from being mentally and emotionally oriented toward life, to being heart or unity centered. As this shift progresses and matures within us, the various conflicting minds within us begin to dissolve and our mind becomes quite silent. Before this shift occurs, we spend most of our lives struggling with the various layers of egoic minds and are unsure how to respond to life from this egoic confusion. Yet after our awakening has matured and included our heart and our gut level of being, we begin to struggle less and less, because all the various aspects of our being: mental, emotional, physical and spiritual come into a full alignment. As this process unfolds, for the first time in our lives, we feel sane and whole. The way that this translates to our practical life is that, all inner conflict dissolves, and the inner dialogue disappears and we are left with a silent, heart centered unity. What we notice is that we rarely have to think much about what to do, in fact the very capacity to *think about* or *figure out life* in an egoic way dissolves and we find ourselves simply responding to life from a space of heart centered silence. At this point, all the egoic voices and minds within us collapse into one mind and we no longer are plagued by a constant stream of never ending inner turmoil due to conflicting aspects of ourselves. In a sense, liberation is about becoming whole, complete and one—inside and out. From this inner unity, what we discover is that *nothing* is outside of or separate from God, even our own mind, thoughts and ego, the very aspects of ourselves that we worked so hard to transcend or get rid of. As our orientation shifts again into unity consciousness, we discover that we are an incarnation of the Divine in every aspect of ourselves, from our thoughts, to our minds, to our egos, to our bodies, to our humanity. We are made in God's image, as God's image, not in any way separate from God in every aspect of ourselves. This Divinity is not some perfected, spiritual divinity but rather, the ordinary radiant perfection of life that includes all experiences—good and bad, big and small, pain and pleasure and every aspect of life seen and unseen. I want to be very clear here: this does not mean that every aspect of our life falls into some total blissful effortless alignment; what I am speaking about is the end of *self created inner turmoil,* we still will have an outer evolving edge in life where we are growing, yet we will see this as Divine—not as a problem that conflicting aspects of our mind fight with. As long as we are humans we will grow in one form or another.

But before this collapse of egoic mentality and the discovery that we are God in every aspect of our being, we have to start where are we are, which means if we are lost in our minds, in the collective unconsciousness, the most compassionate thing we can do is to learn to navigate through the various layers of ego or mind, so that we can respond to life in a sane way. Ultimately this teaching, as well as all teachings, will dissolve in our total completion and Enlightenment. In the meantime, it can be helpful to understand the conflicting insanity of the human experience, so that we can recognize it and are not fooled by it, and so that we are then able to navigate through it in a healthy and sane way. To step into this sanity, it is important to understand the various minds within us, so that we can be mindful of which thoughts are arising from which mind within us. If we know where our thoughts are coming from, we can decide if we want to listen to a particular voice or not. For example, if we can consciously see that the space of our awareness is filled with emotional thoughts, then we can choose in the present moment not to listen to these thoughts, but instead to be rational about what is arising within us. We may like the idea of a new car or a large bowl of ice cream, but if we are mindful we choose to respond to life with wisdom. Instead of reacting to life impulsively or emotionally, we can choose to instead, respond with the intelligence of our rational mind, which in most cases will be the smarter choice. Furthermore, with mindfulness, we can even choose to not to respond from either of these minds (emotional or rational) but instead, respond from the innate wisdom of our hearts. In fact, the more we respond from the wisdom of our hearts the deeper we will embody our own innate Divinity, which is omniscient. As we choose to respond from the wisdom of our heart, we tap into the all knowing brilliance of the universe.

But to be able to discern between the voice of our hearts and the voice of our minds, we have to understand each voice and know it intimately. To do this requires mindfulness or the ability to step out of our minds and observe what is arising. When we become mindful of what we think and where our thoughts are arising from, our relationship with what we think radically changes, because we take the wind out of the sails of our egoic mentality. We can shift from being used by our minds to *using* our minds. To be able to make this shift into mindfulness and the power of our choice, it is helpful to first fully understand the various layers of mind, so that we can discern what is arising and from where, and we can then choose to respond in an empowered way.

The Mental Mind

The mental mind is commonly thought of as the rational mind in our head. In its most healthy state it is a very rational, discerning tool. It could be used to compute or to quickly decide what is the most efficient way home from work or who would be a good friend to take rock climbing and it may quickly discern if an activity such as rock climbing is safe. This type of mentality, most people do not struggle with unless they are highly emotional, lost in victimhood or painfully struggling in life. The mental mind in its most healthy state can be very much like rational computer. A good example of this healthy mentality is how an accountant uses their mind to balance books or how a carpenter uses their mind to build a house. But it is a rare individual who uses their mind in this way in every area of their life. When we are free, we can *choose* to use our mind to work for us in a healthy, practical way. We can do this because we are living outside of the collective insanity and chaos of our minds, and can choose to use our mind in a sane, practical way, instead of being *used* by our mind. Unfortunately most of us are used by our minds, because our mind has so many unhealthy programs running out of control within it, very much like a malicious computer virus. These programs can, for example, come in the form of unhealthy belief systems or radical ideologies or emotional wounds. Because of these unhealthy programs within us, even when we exercise our will and try to shut the program off, it continues to pop up in our consciousness and runs despite our efforts to stop it. For most of humanity this experience is a normal everyday occurrence. It is no wonder why our world is so out of control.

Our rational mind becomes unhealthy or clouded by all of the unhealthy programs we pick up from life. For instance, one major program that our collective mind has is the program that is constantly searching and scanning the world or environment for danger or problems. Essentially, the mind is always gently scanning the environment for problems in order to keep us safe. Yet if we grew up in a difficult environment, this mind or program kept us safe from harm. Yet after time, this program will become conditioned by this experience of constantly being defensive and will begin to assume that the world or life is not safe. It will then continue on autopilot scanning and looking for problems constantly and will continue, even when we have moved on to a safe environment. So if we identify with this mind and give it free range to operate, it will quickly find a problem with our partners, our parents, our friends, our job, our car, our situation, and sadly ourselves. It is helpful to know and understand that the mind looks for problems automatically, and if we have had a tough life or have experienced trauma that our mind will look for problems in a hyperactive way. If we take the time to heal our past pain or egoic conditioning with love, our mind will be able to calm down and will then gently do its job in a normal way. Yet, when we wake up to our undivided nature, we learn that we will be much happier, if we do not listen to this mind at all, unless it is a matter of safety or if something *really* needs our attention. If there is any doubt about this program within us, we can try this exercise: In the morning as we wake up, we can simply notice the first thought of the day and notice if it is a problem of some form. *I wish I didn't have to go to work, damn it is early, or cold, or I'm late, the alarm is loud etc*. We all have received this critical and defensive *program* from evolution in order to keep us safe. Yet because most of us live in a relatively safe world most of the time, most of us do not need to listen to this hypersensitive or critical program ninety five percent of the time.

Layered on top of our rational computer-like mind are many different programs, one of the main programs we just discussed; but there are thousands of other programs layered on top of this mind. Some are our belief systems about life, politics, relationships or work. Some we picked up from our culture, or our gender, many we inherited from our parents and family. It is helpful to note that many of these, if not all of these programs we simply picked up from our experience of life—almost like a malicious internet virus that we unconsciously downloaded while surfing the internet. These programs are completely impersonal, and just downloaded themselves into us and do not necessarily have any inherent truth within them, yet most of us are willing to fight for these very programs or beliefs within us, because we have unconsciously identified with them as part of our identity.

Many of us have had the experience of being accused of acting like our parents in a negative way and instead of humbly admitting to this and working to heal this habitual nature of mind that was passed on to us, we defend ourselves, arguing with the accusations, while being in the present moment, a manifestation of our parents programming. When we are free or wake up to our true nature, we discover that these programs which we took to be ourselves, are impersonal and have nothing to do with us. We discover that they are simply a layer of collective consciousness which we wear on top of our true identity. Yet most of the world mistakes this cloak for themselves and as a result greatly suffer. When we are awake enough to reflect on our thoughts, our beliefs, and our behaviors we can then choose to live beyond them, if we first meet them with love and friendliness.

If we really examine this truth, we might actually begin to ask, *what am I? What am I beyond these programs, that aren't even really me?* We can use our rational mind to inquire in this way. Yet it takes discipline to use our rational mind for inquiry and not be seduced by this very mind or conditioning. Sometimes it is helpful to write out our inquiry process, so that we can see our thoughts, and examine them outside of ourselves. As we write down our thoughts and beliefs, we can question each one in a very precise way. We can ask *is this thought or belief true? How do I know? Do I know this is true with 100% certainty? Where did this thought come from? Did I pick this up from my parents, or my school or my culture?* Quickly we will discover that most of what we believe is a repetition of what we were taught or given by our upbringing or an opinion or an assumption or a projection based on our interpretation of the past—not the *truth*. Truth is not an opinion of what should or should not happen, truth is *what is happening* beyond the movement of our repetitive conditioned beliefs about life.

It is important to be disciplined while we inquire into our beliefs. Our minds are so seductive that we can become seduced by a thought in a millisecond, even during the inquiry process. Countless times, I have inquired deeply into something without having a discipline and a few minutes later, I find myself thinking about something quite unrelated; this is the nature of mind. I find it so helpful to write my process of inquiry down on paper, so that we are not taken on a ride in our mind. Putting it in writing can really help with this discipline so that we can begin to separate *ourselves* from what we *think*, so we can separate truth from our beliefs, opinions and projections. As we do engage in the process of inquiry, we begin to discover who we are not, and ultimately who we are beyond our imagined sense of self.

Emotional Mind

Beyond being mindful of and inquiring into the nature of our mental minds, we can also deeply examine our emotional minds. The emotional mind can be just as challenging for us as our mental minds, if not more. The emotional mind lives within our torso, in the area between our throat and our pelvis. We all know what it *feels* like in our body when we are deeply sad, enraged or fully feeling wonderful. It is no doubt that our emotional mind arises out of our body. We literally *feel* the emotional thoughts in our body. Many individuals try very hard to not listen to their emotions and in some cases resort to painful means to suppress this energy within themselves. Because it is so common to suppress emotions, many individuals have a hard time getting in touch with them. But despite many of the social and cultural norms for suppressing emotions, being mindful of our emotions is quite natural and leads to greater sanity and happiness, if we are willing to be courageous enough *to feel* what is here.

Our emotional thoughts are quite easy to become conscious of because we *feel* them so fully; they tend to be loud and get our attention in our body. To become aware of these feelings, it is necessary for us to pull our awareness out of our minds and bring our attention to the present-felt sensations in our bodies and notice *fully*, what we are feeling. When we simply give ourselves permission to feel, we open ourselves to the world of our emotional mind. Many emotions are right there waiting for us to listen, feel and experience them. But if we live all of our lives only in our mental minds, these emotions stay stuck or repressed in our bodies as they simmer. Yet while these unexpressed emotions are simmering, the energetic vibrations of these emotions make their way into our mental minds and effect the way we think. This repression fuels most of our neurotic thoughts, feelings, beliefs and behaviors.

Some of our emotions are right on or just below the surface of our consciousness and are easily felt and experienced when we become mindful of our feelings. Also, there lies a whole world of unconscious emotions, thoughts, drives, desires, and wounds that are constantly yet subtly working in the background of our present reality. These unconscious thoughts drive much of our behavior, even though we are mostly unaware of them. Freud wrote volumes on these drives and spent a lifetime investigating these forces within us. We may notice them as we walk into a room and sit next to someone who is beautiful because we are attracted to them or because we feel safe. We may unconsciously scowl at our boss or our partner without even knowing it. To be mindful is to be courageous enough to willingly examine these drives within us and choose which to respond to and which to let go.

If we just had one mind, most of us would be better able to live in a relative amount of sanity, but because we have many minds within us, we become fragmented quite quickly, especially when the different minds are in opposition to each other. What is really confusing is that our mental mind may be saying one thing, and our emotional mind may be saying something else. This is the common human experience of being divided, which is opposite of *being unified* or *whole*, which is what we experience as we step out of our minds and into freedom. We all know the common experience being divided and inwardly confused, when our relationship with someone ends. Our mental mind may say *we need to go* and our emotional mind, may say, *we need to get back together*. Conflicting thoughts are a common experience of being a human; this conflict of being inwardly divided is essentially, the root of suffering. Yet, the opposite can also be true as well, if our mental and emotional minds and our heart agree, we feel unity and clarity. Even when we are working with a tough decision, if we are in alignment with the intelligence of our heart, there will be a feeling of *rightness* about our decision. Our experience of life energetically will *feel truer,* if we are acting from our hearts, than if we were simply acting from one of our various egoic minds. Yet, this does not necessarily mean our experience will be painless. Our egoic mind is always looking for the pain free option, yet our hearts will do what is true, despite how it feels. Pain in life is inevitable, but how we relate to pain is our choice. If we choose to meet life with truth and openness it may still hurt, but we will not be deluded by our minds.

One of the most difficult aspects of the emotional mind are the wounds that live within the emotional mind. These are deeply buried pains within us that often arise in the present when someone or something reminds us of our past pain. A common example is when we were a child and did not receive the love that we needed; this wound may flare up or be invoked when we do not experience the love we want in our adult life. If we were denied love as a child, and then later on as an adult we are let down by a friend or partner, the original wound or pain may be activated, and we may react to life or the current situation with an unusual amount of emotion. Another common example of this might be, that we were teased as a child for something we said, so we become shy and have trouble speaking up for ourselves later on in life. These wounds live in us unconsciously, until we become mindful of them and fully validate and feel the unexpressed original emotion and allow it to release from our body. Unless we do this courageous work, our feelings will continue to cause us so much suffering in our present lives.

These wounds can be so powerful that they can override our healthy, rational minds. Often these wounds can be greater than our will power, which is why stuffing or repressing emotions deep in our bodies does not work; eventually they find their way to the surface because they want to be healed. Often these wounds need to be fully met with nothing short of total loving kindness and acceptance, before they can heal and release from our consciousness. This is where therapy or a healing professional can be greatly helpful in supporting us to grieve the original pain or wound and assist us in moving toward healing.

The emotional mind at its most primitive level is driven by the desire for what feels good and to avoid pain. There are times when it is absolutely appropriate to listen to this voice and other times when listening to this voice will lead to an absolute nightmare. Most individuals have no training or education on how to work with this powerful mind within in us. Ironically many of us view our emotions as childish and immature, yet at the same time, many of us make our major decisions from this place. Even the most aware individuals often give way to the emotional voice within. Throughout history many great individuals have chosen to listen to this emotional voice, and it has lead to incredible suffering. Many find the emotional mind the most difficult to work with because, this mind *feels* so powerful. Yet emotional storms often leave us quickly, if we are willing to acknowledge and feel the storms fully in the moment they arise. This requires that we meet them with an absolute loving kindness and acceptance. But if we instead deny these feelings, they can simmer for years, while deeply affecting our behavior and belief systems often in an unconscious and neurotic way.

Making decisions from this emotional mind often will lead us out of clarity and into a deeper delusion. If we are going to act from freedom or clarity we must be willing to discern the truth of our hearts, from the feeling and story that comes with our emotional mind. If we are going to listen to the truth of our hearts, the way something *feels* is not the most important deciding factor. If we are going to live in the truth, we must be willing to know what is in our hearts and to choose to act from this place. If we look back at our lives, there have been many times when something felt powerful and we were drawn in that direction and chose to go, but we later painfully discovered that this choice caused so much suffering for us and those around us. Most individuals who have been involved in an affair describe how good it felt initially, yet admit regrettably, how much pain they caused. We can all think of times in our life, when we were swayed by powerful feelings and ended up in the wrong place, with painful consequences. Again with mindfulness, we can examine our feelings and decide if we are going to act on our feelings or let them pass through our body, without acting them out. But without mindfulness, we are unconsciously driven by our unexamined feelings and suffer the consequences and continue to live in the world of illusion.

If we consider freedom our highest value, it does not matter how we *feel*. This can come as quite a shock to our emotional minds, where its whole basis is built on *feeling the best for its own sake*. We can quickly see the arrogance and egoic self-centeredness of our emotional mind. To support our emotional mind's desire to feel good at all costs, our mental mind will often join in and support the argument or story.

The mental mind can arise at lightning speed, and create an argument defending the case. When we step out of our minds and see what is happening, it can be quite humbling to see how quickly our mind can manipulate and shape shift. At this moment we can again ask, *am I this mind, or am I the one that sees the mind? Can I be mindful of what is happening within me and not be fooled into believing my own mind's movements?* This can be quite difficult or challenging, if we try to be mindful while strong emotions flare up and are supported by our mental mind's arguments. As this dance of mind happens, even if we have a moment of insight about what is happening, we can still experience a deep pull back into our delusion. But if we are going to be free, we must be willing to stand our ground and not give into these feelings. This is really what the spiritual path is all about—the willingness to live beyond the conditioned mental and emotional minds. If we make this step beyond feeling *good* and thinking we are *right,* it can be quite thrilling, and liberating and is the very doorway to our freedom.

Physical mind

Beyond our mental and emotional minds are our physical minds. The physical mind includes the mind of our physical body, its basic needs, habits, addictions, strengths, weaknesses, cravings, aversions, and relationship to life. This mind is the most basic and primitive but can give us a great deal of strength and/or trouble depending on how it has been trained or treated by us and our life. Many of us struggle with physical addictions or cravings and this mind also has its own agenda, which is to seek pleasure and avoid pain, and is quite similar to our emotional mind in this way. This voice of our physical mind can add another layer of confusion, or a wonderful support to us. This mind is simple, yet important for our stability. It constantly is making sure that our basic needs are met and that we are kept safe. If we deny these needs our whole system can begin to get off track, shut down or go haywire. It does not matter if we are awake to our true nature or asleep at the wheel, if we deny our physical needs such as not sleeping or not eating or not taking care of our health, we will soon be greatly humbled by this mind. If we deny ourselves our basic needs, we may find an animal-like consciousness coming forward that will do anything to take care of itself. That being said, it is an act of love to treat our physicality with the utmost respect and care.

One of the reasons people exercise, hike or practice yoga is that it gets us in touch with the quiet strength of this mind. Because this mind is so simple, it is also very silent. Many people practice yoga and have no idea why they like it so much. Upon investigation, it is often seen that when we drop out of our mental and emotional minds and concentrate on our physical bodies, these other minds calm down. When we get out of our heads, we notice the quiet that is here within us all the time. Even if we experience pain in our bodies, and just see or feel the pain from the simplicity of physical mind, without having a big story around it, it may begin to open and release. This mind seems to have a simple intelligence and openness to it. Getting in touch with this aspect of our self can be quite a relief from the normal turmoil of our mental and emotional minds. This is possible when we can simply drop into our bodies and notice what is within us, without engaging in our mental or emotional stories of the past or hopes and dreams of the future.

The unhealthy version of this mind can be seen in our unconscious cravings or our fight or flight response to life. If we pick up a habit such as smoking or using drugs, the physical mind of our body can quickly become addicted to the substance and then very loudly demand that we have this substance on a daily or hourly basis. Our rational mind may know clearly that these substances are dangerous for us to take, but this physical mind if addicted, does not care, and will continue to ingest the substance even if it leads us to our own death. It may require great effort or surrender to end this dance with addiction. Our physical mind may scream, shout and even steal so that it can have the substance it is addicted to. But deep in our heart we know that this is not the way to live. We may experience a similar dance in relationship to our sexual desire; we can make very foolish mistakes when we are caught in the grips of physical desire. Many great and even enlightened sages have fallen on their faces in the wake of sexual desire. When the overwhelming creative and attractive energies of the universe, which is essentially what sexual desire is, mixes with our physical mind, we can literally go crazy and make great fools of ourselves and cause tremendous pain. This energy, as well as the energies of power and anger, can be some of the most difficult energies to work with in our minds. If we find ourselves struggling with these energies, it is necessary to have a vast perspective of mindfulness as these energies come and go through our minds and bodies. Because the power of these energies are so strong and the consequences that come with these energies are so great; it is absolutely essential that we do not become seduced by these energies or great karma will be created. Instead if we want to be free, we will identify with the vastness of our consciousness and allow this energy to pass through our being without acting on it, unless of course these energies are in complete alignment with our heart. While working with these energies they may literally rage through our bodies, yet, if we are courageous, we will breathe through this experience and allow it to pass, which may take a moment or even weeks. We may literally need to lie down and allow these energies to surge and rage through our bodies. It is important for us not to fear these feelings and sensations. If we fear these feelings, chances are we will act out these very energies. Yet if we see them for what they are and allow this experience to surge through our body without acting on them and without believing the terrifying or seductive thoughts that come with these energies, we will be free. This can be quite tricky, because when we are facing these powerful forces of nature and mind, our minds may provide a very convincing rationale, and entice us with wonderful feelings if we act on our desire or we may experience very real, yet often imagined fears if we do not act. This is our moment to be vast and stay put where we are. As this storm moves through us, it would be wise for us to drop into the depths of our hearts and decide from our hearts how to proceed. If we fail to listen to our heart and instead listen to these powerful feelings and act upon them, there is the potential for incredible suffering.

Often in the spiritual world we have learned that the mind is something to get rid of. But all of these minds can be wonderful tools and supports for us in the world. If we meet their basic needs of safety and love, they tend to run smoothly. If we deny, ignore or stuff their needs, they tend to act up or cry out for our attention. If we respond with a universal friendliness to these various aspects within us, we tend to heal and mature. If we ignore them out of fear or transcend them with our spirituality, our evolution will stagnate or we may become neurotic. But if we want to be sane and have a mind that operates clearly, we need to spend a great deal of time working with our minds in the places that do not operate smoothly. As we do this work, our mind becomes our ally and is no longer our foe.

The disappearance of the personal will

To live and embody our fullest expression of our awakened Divinity, it is necessary to continue to investigate the various parts of our self where we continue to become deluded and uproot and heal these places within us, so that we can live free of their power over us. In order to *stay* awake and grow in our expression of our Divinity, it is necessary to continually investigate our relationship with our personal egoic conditioning and the collective unconsciousness. Our personal will, which is one of the fundamental building blocks of ego, is one of the major places within us where we quickly become unconscious or lost in egoic identification. Our will, which is located in the depths of our gut, is most basically, the psychological force or program within us that wants to survive, maintain, assert itself, fight against, or fundamentally separate itself in order to create a separate sense of identity. Most individuals are so identified with their will that they cannot even conceive of who they would be without this fundamental drive to exist as a separate egoic identity. Because of this deep attachment and identification with our wills, most of humanity would find it difficult to even become mindful of this aspect of ego.

Yet if we take a moment to step out of our mentality, we can begin to notice this impersonal force within us. If we bring our attention to our abdomen, we may notice a slight tension in the depths of our abdomen about two inches below our belly button and a few inches below the surface of our skin. We can experiment with this investigation by thinking of a time when someone personally attacked us or by remembering something that we are deeply angry about. We may notice that we now feel a clenching or resistance within the depths of our abdomen; this is the movement of our will. In a healthy way, our will is the desire behind what makes us want to have a career or have a family or be a part of a political party and our will is also, what drives us to succeed at sports or want to be "right." From a psychological perspective, a good strong egoic will create a healthy sense of self from which an individual can operate in the world. Paradoxically when we *awaken from* our personal egoic will, we experience a period of time when we have no real desire for anything. For the first time in our lives we may have no ideas or opinions about anything. We may have no desire to go here or there. During this period of the *dissolving of our will* we may experience incredible emptiness, which may be tremendously liberating for some, or almost depressing for others. This period may last a month or for years, until this emptiness is one day filled with the Divine Will. The Divine Will is experienced as an incredible, dynamic and creative power within us, that comes with a feeling of a *fearless sanity*. It is a rare individual who has awakened or surrendered this deeply, and allowed God's Will to become their will. Most of the individuals on the path, even those who are "awake," still deeply struggle with their egoic will.

If we *believe* too much in our egoic will or take it too seriously, and mistake our will for who and what we truly are, this will lead us to greater suffering. We all have known times when we have fought persistently to be right and, as a result, experienced intense separation and suffering. If we give our will too much power or authority over ourselves, we will end up believing exclusively in its/our point of view. This point of view is generally some version of *me against the world*. If we see the world from this perspective of separation, we will not be seeing Life from the nonperspective of Unity, of Oneness.

Naturally our relationship with our will must be investigated, if we are going to be free. There are many spiritual practices and ascetic techniques that work to break down our will such as, hours and hours of meditation and difficult yogic asanas. Many spiritual traditions prescribe difficult labor without any purpose or aim, such as racking gravel in one direction and then the other direction to break our will. Our will, will absolutely argue with these ridiculous tasks or efforts, until when one day, it finally breaks down. I have participated in countless retreats where we would sit all day in meditation, I have done silly things like traveling to India and getting up at 3.30 in the morning to sit in hours of meditation, and can admit that this type of practice was semi-successful in helping to bring my will to a place of surrender. But I find that Life does a much better job at breaking us down and opening us up. Although, these spiritual practices can be helpful if done with sincerity, this is not always the case. If these practices are performed by relying on our egoic will power, they can actually reinforce the will, not exhaust it. Though if we are sincere in our practices, a wonderful space opens when we give up our fight, after our will has become exhausted from trying so hard to make life work for us, and we become so open and raw that we have no choice but to surrender. This is where most spiritual practices try to bring us, to this point of exhaustion and eventual surrender. Although, we are welcome at any point to fully surrender our will and to let go, right here, right now without being exhausted, without our difficult spiritual practices; we are welcome to instead surrender to Life in each and every moment. This is the direct path; to step onto the direct path, we must be deeply sincere, and be more sincere than our attachment to our own will. Sincere surrender is by far the most direct way to let go of the will and to step into this huge Mystery that we are.

We will all notice that one day at some point along our journey, the will naturally begins to break and exhaust itself. It may happen before, during or after awakening. Many seekers on the path have huge shifts in consciousness after letting go and deeply surrendering their will; yet what is more often the case is that the Divine comes and without us knowing, simply begins to take our will and leaving us speechless as a result. When we let go of a major aspect of our egoic identity or *when it is taken from us*, we will naturally begin to awaken to our innate undivided Divinity, which is always present yet covered by our egoic tendencies. This uncovering of our Divinity is a process, not something that happens all at once. Our will has many layers and like anything on the path, we may see the emergence or disappearance of one layer, which at the time may feel like a complete shift into our Divinity, but we may then notice that our will reasserts itself again or a deeper layer of it comes forward and we reidentify with it. During this process of transition and growth, we may become frustrated because our wonderful spiritual identity may disappear for some time as our egoic sense of self resurrects itself. Rather than becoming frustrated, we could *choose* to become inclusive and see that another part of our egoic identity has come forward to be transformed or to be surrendered. In this way, we do not fight against the process of awakening—a process that will eventually make its way to every part of our being. We are essentially invited to be open to every part of ourselves growing, healing and expanding or dissolving as long as we are here on earth.

In a practical way, we may notice that if we find ourselves to be tense or tight in our being, chances are that our will is present fighting or arguing with Reality. Our invitation is to surrender and open to the tightness and tension present and again, we are invited to let go into our spacious nature. We may find ourselves at one moment open and free of ego, and in the next moment, a deeper part of our will may come forward into this very openness that we are, to be surrendered. If we want to stay awake, we must be willing to surrender to this process of continued growth fully and continually at each step in our evolution.

This whole experience of letting go of our will can be quite disorienting or terrifying, because we are letting go of the very thing we existentially identified with as *us*. There may be times when our will may greatly diminish or disappear, leaving us feeling open and spacious yet confused about how to function or confused about what we want because nothing seems to matter anymore. Because our will is the very thing within us that wants, needs and asserts itself, when our will diminishes, we may be left with a feeling of not having any desire for *this* or *that* or that we have no desire to do anything at all. Most of us have never experienced this in our lives. If suddenly we find that we do not know what we want, it can be very confusing. We may not know what to do with ourselves, what to say or how to respond, because our old way of being is absent or dissolving from our sense of self. We may find in situations where in the past, we were drawn into drama and gossip, that now we no longer have any desire to engage in life in this way. We may realize that our political party is not going to save the world and that we no longer are passionate about our political agenda. This does not mean that we stop voting, we may still vote; but we realize that if our candidate loses the election that Life will be fully ok, no matter what happens. This shift occurs because our egoic identity begins to dissolve as we embrace a trust in the intelligence of Life, and further, allow ourselves to become this very Intelligence, by living in accordance with it.

I have always been really driven in life and known what I wanted. When I was first taught meditation, I was the kind of guy who would sit in meditation for three hours a day, every single day for years. And beyond my earlier years of intense meditation practice, I have literally not missed a single day of meditation in 20 years—I always had a strong will and greatly relied on it, until paradoxically this will, one day began to vanish. As my will began to dissolve, I at first, became really frightened as I had no idea what was happening to me; everything seemed in one sense absolutely perfect and yet, I had no idea how to go forward or where my will, that I had once relied on for so many years, went. I didn't know what to do with myself. Also during this time, much of my work and income began to fall away. I often became very frightened that I would not be able to pay my bills. I knew that I had to continue to go to work, because I had children to take care of, but had difficulty finding any meaningful work. I began to have this paradoxical experience of my ego flaring up and becoming terrified and yet I no longer seemed to care about all the things that I normally cared about. I could care less about the news and the politics that I held so dearly, I could care less about wanting my parents to change, I could care less about what people thought of me, I no longer cared to argue with anyone. It was very disorienting to go from having so many agendas about life and for others, to not having any agendas beyond paying the bills and taking care of my kids. If I saw a psychologist, they probably would have labeled me as dissociated, but I actually experienced such a wonderful intimacy with life and was so happy, that I would not have met the diagnosis. When we are dissociated we don't care and lack feeling, which is quite different than actually waking up and letting go of our will. My agendas had disappeared, which left me feeling free, and I experienced an overwhelming love and intimacy with life; this shift of letting go of my agendas for life left me overwhelmed by the very Beauty of Life. It was a small price to pay, to discover the absolute Beauty of the universe in my everyday waking reality.

This can be a very confusing transition because so much of our egoic identity is our will. Our ego gets its identity from wanting and striving and doing. If this disappears, we may find ourselves quite dumbfounded. Someone may ask us, "what do we want to do?" And we may have no idea. At first this may seem bizarre, but this is quite normal to experience as we give up our petty agendas and make way for something greater. If we want to be free, we must be willing to walk into this great unknown and *be* this unknown on a gut level. This shift may come with a great realization that none of it really matters—that most of what we worry about isn't worth the price we pay for worrying. This of course is such a relief as we fully allow everything to be as it is. We discover that it does not matter what color we paint the room or if someone steps on our toes or if we get a speeding ticket or if a family member decides not to talk to us. We stop taking life personally. In a sense, almost everything becomes ok, because there is no *one* here to argue. This is quite different than living in the normal collective consciousness, where everyone is lost in their egoic wants, needs, and agendas. For those of us whose *wants* and *desires* are our identity, this transition may be painful, because we are letting go of our very identity. More accurately, our identity *is falling away* and when this happens, our ego may become confused, disoriented or may desperately grasp at this dissolving identity, yet if we can trust that this is all part of the process, this dissolving can become no big deal. If we stop going into work because we no longer care about our job or find no meaning in it and have no plan what to do next, we will probably experience feelings of terror and confusion, but this too may be ok, and yet, not very practical. When I look back on this process, I see that it was such a beautiful time for me. I spent a lot of time lying on the couch on my back porch staring at the trees, and the sky, as various elements of my ego faded away. Yet I can still remember the sinking feeling in my gut and the stress that would come when I realized I had no money and rent was due. I can also remember the feeling of being alone and simply wanting some help. Being alone was probably the most difficult experience for me during this time. I deeply wanted someone to hold my hand through this process, and many people did show up along the way and took care of me in one way or another. Yet ultimately I was on my own, and I discovered an amazing trust and support from Life, that I may not have experienced had I not been alone.

We all know that people with the biggest egos are also the most difficult to be around, because they always have an idea, a comment, an agenda that they are imposing on the world. When we lose our will, we don't really care anymore about most of the nonsense that previously busied our minds. We give up arguing with Reality. We give up wanting things to be different. We give up wanting our parents to switch political parties. We give up wanting to be right. In a sense we let everything be as it is. This is freedom, when we can allow everything to be as it is, without having to fix, or amend life. Not many want this type of freedom. Most of us want to get what we want, which is egoic freedom. Egoic freedom is more like the freedom of the millionaire who gets to meet all of their wants, needs and agendas. But spiritual freedom comes when we allow everything to be as it is and are content and happy with whatever our outward circumstances are. Ironically, when we deeply let go and allow Life to be, we become fully available for Life to show up in whatever way Life asks of us. In comparison, the ego asks or demands life to serve us.

This transition from an egoic way of existing to being fully awake to Life, may be huge and dramatic or subtle and simple, but either way, we may find ourselves not sure what to do with ourselves, as our egoic attachments dissolve and nothing seems to matter anymore. If our shift in consciousness happens to be on the more dramatic side and we lose our will all at once, we may find ourselves spellbound in this vast open transcendent world and see the world of the mind and ego as completely meaningless. This can be quite shocking and disorienting to our being. During these times it can be quite helpful to have a teacher or a guide, to help us become grounded and be able to function in the world in a wise and practical way.

If we begin to experience life as meaningless, it would be incorrect to assume that because life *feels* meaningless or unimportant that it actually *is* meaningless. There is quite a difference between a dissociated, meaningless indifference and connecting to Life in a non-egoic way. The difference is the feeling or experience of intimacy. Life may not care what color we paint our room, but does *care* if while we paint, we are intimate with the act of painting, with those around us, and with all of life as a whole.

What many of us miss on the spiritual path is that Life or the world of form *is* the Divine. What we need to learn is how to have a right relationship with Life and embrace and include all of Life. Many seekers unconsciously do not want to be a part of life and seek to transcend life, but the point of the spiritual journey in not to avoid life. If the point were to transcend life, then we might as well be homeless or couch surfers living off everyone else and not engage in life in any way. Yet God is the vast spaciousness of the universe and is also the dynamic energy of creation. When we awaken to the transcendent we identify with the vast spaciousness, yet if we stop here and do not engage in life, we only realize half of the truth. God did not put us here on this planet to deny Life or renounce it, or to transcend it, God put us here to awaken to ourselves and engage ourselves in a dynamic way in accordance with Her perfection and will.

We are here to do something much greater than to satisfy the desires of our ego and we often have no idea what this will look like. For most of us before we awaken, we just have *ideas* of what the disillusionment of our will might look like. As it begins to happen, our egos become terrified because as we lose our identities it may feel like a kind of death. And we may have all these ideas that our world will fall apart, if we are no longer trying to control it or we may fear that because we are letting go of our perceived sense of control that we won't take care of our practical needs. As an example, for me it was the fear of letting go of control and not being able to pay the bills. Yet ironically, we can let go of our perceived sense of control and still show up to work. For anyone who goes through this transition, it may manifest as intense fears of losing control, because for the first time in our lives we are letting go of our *perceived* sense of control over life. We may experience fears of losing our jobs or our relationships. But the opposite actually happens; we become freed up from our own egocentricity and find, surprisingly, that we are able to meet life more *fully* and paradoxically in an unattached way. Yet, during this transition we may lose a job or a career or relationship. I lost them all and was given so much more in return. I was given an overwhelming joy, love and deep trust in life, and began to see that I was *the very thing I was seeking.*

During this transition, many folks become scared that they are going to stop caring about the important things, because one of the primary functions of our will is to tend to what we think *is* most important to us. But we can remember we that are not surrendering to or giving control over to another ego or a reckless force, we are surrendering control over to the Divine Intelligence of Life Itself, *which has always been in control anyway.* This can be such an incredible relief to realize this, and quite comical at the same time. This is the great cosmic joke. We surrender to God, even though God has always been in charge and we experience a great relief from no longer fighting with God about how life should be. And when we give up this fight, suddenly all of our egoic energy that was fighting against the movement of Life can now fall into alignment with Life. On a human level this experience is tremendously energizing. In a sense, we become freed from all the nonsense and things we couldn't control and give ourselves deeply to the movement of Life in a total way. We become more empowered to give and to act because we are not busy arguing with all the petty things in life.

I was once in line at a coffee shop in Oakland, trying to get a cup of tea on my way to see Adya speak. As I waited in line, I noticed something quite hilarious. One by one, each of the customers gave their most neurotic and egocentric performances. Each individual would place their order with such exact detail about how they wanted their personalized coffee drink made. I found this very entertaining as I waited my turn. Right before I ordered, the person next in line, a young and deeply determined man, put his two hands down on the counter and looked the barista in the eye with such intensity about his order. He acted as though, if his order was not made precisely correct, that he might die. At that moment, I had to laugh and leave, I couldn't contain myself. I saw myself in this young man, and how silly I had been over the smallest things, let alone something really important. To this day, I am amazed that there is a multibillion dollar industry built on people getting their coffee exactly as their ego wants. For so much of our lives, we often act like we are two year olds in adult bodies having our tantrums over petty things, while missing the vast beauty that surrounds us. How funny we all are.

When we let go of our will, it does not matter what life brings us. It does not matter if things do not go perfectly according to our plan. Instead, we align with *what is happening* and take what comes as the Divine, Herself. We all know that the people who are the easiest to be around are those who go with the flow of Life; they happily go with the flow, because their will or ego has relaxed and surrendered. In this moment we can inquire into our relationship with life. We can begin to look within at our relationship to our will. Is it strong or is it weak? Have we relaxed and surrendered? Or are there places within where we are still holding onto things that do not serve us? Can we be open to loving these places within that are still fighting and gently begin to let go? Can we see, that within the fear or terror of letting go, is our freedom, is our power? Can we remind ourselves that we are letting go into God, not into death? For when we surrender to the will of the Divine, we are given new life.

In the beginning of the path, a strong will can be quite helpful. We may need a strong will to encourage and support our discipline to practice. We may engage this will to keep us out of trouble. A weak will leads to laziness and inertia, or being like a ping pong ball doing whatever the environment stimulates us to do. In a sense, if we have no backbone, life will push us around and we will fall prey to every unconscious movement in our environment. We have all experienced moments in our lives of this. But it is good to be clear that letting go of our will is not in any way the same as having a weak will. Letting go of our will means we are willing to let something higher than our ego guide us. As we do so, we may find ourselves not caring if we receive the wrong milk in our coffee or if we hear someone gossip about us. Yet, we will begin to know how to act when something deep comes our way. And when we finally let go fully, the action will just come out of us, without any thought or effort, while we are simultaneously, humbly amazed by the supreme Intelligence of it all.

End of conflict

As we wake up, the very fabric of our mind begins to change and we begin to see and experience oneness all around us with an overwhelming intimacy. Our vision of life changes so that as we look out at life we no longer see and experience separation, but instead we begin to see and feel a radiant Beauty everywhere we find ourselves. As our vision shifts from seeing life from a place of survival and separation, to one of Love and Unity, we start to directly experience this Unity throughout our being; and as a result there is an intuitive and experiential knowing that we and everything we see is Divine, and that this Divinity, this ineffable beauty runs throughout all of Life. This is what I call the doorway of liberation.

As we grow in this vision and it becomes greater and more stable within us, we begin to see that there is no thing in Life is which is not Divine. This does not mean that life is not difficult or brutal; but paradoxically, our vision grows in a way that sees that what we once thought of as good and bad are *both* Divine. But to realize this, our definition of Divinity must change from an egoic definition of divinity that only includes things that are heavenly, holy and *what feels good*, to a total definition of Divinity that includes everyone and everything, all experiences, worlds, levels and *all* of life—even the insanity, pain, brutality, death and destruction of life.

As we awaken into this new way of seeing, all judgments and conflicts begin to fall away as we realize everything to be Divine. We begin to ask ourselves, *how could anything be outside of God?* God created this world and put all the events in motion, so what could there be that is not Divine? As the awakening process deepens, we shift from interpreting and judging reality based on how we feel, to seeing all of life as the movement of God, despite what our mind may think or feel about it. As we shift into this greater and more inclusive perspective, we intuitively begin to see that there is an intelligence that runs the universe and that we are all simultaneously evolving toward wholeness and unity, despite the negativity and pain that is experienced in life. We begin to see that all of life is a movement of evolution. Some areas of life are moving at lower or more primitive levels of evolution, whereas other areas of life are evolving with more inclusive and compassionate manifestations. Yet all of it is the Divine.

Although, if we are honest we can fully admit that there are many things in life that we do not understand with our human minds, especially war, natural disaster and the brutality of life. It will always be the case, that we don't mentally know why there is incredible suffering in the world. Yet despite not mentally or intellectually knowing why life is the way it is, we come to intuitively recognize that there is an inherent Goodness that runs through the fabric of creation. As this recognition and vision grows within us, many of our everyday conflicts begin to dissolve within, because we begin to see and experience the awakened vision of Unity and Love throughout our lives. The True awakened vision is not dependent on how we feel or getting what we want, nor is it found through prolonging a spiritual experience. Many of us can enjoy an experience of awakening as long as we feel good and are getting what we want. Yet not many of us can embody this vision that the world is Divine while we feel bad or have to accept that we are not getting what we want. When things go our way, our ego relaxes and drops its defensive walls and as these walls drop, we naturally experience unity and love. Yet how many of us, can embody this vision of Divinity, while the world angers and upsets our humanness? If we can stay open in these difficult moments, we will remain free. But if we cannot, then our invitation is to accept that we don't always get our way, and give ourselves full permission to laugh or cry and then again awaken to the Beauty that is here, even if we do not get our way in each and every moment. At some point, when we eventually become so deeply comfortable in ourselves, we will begin to see Love no matter what is happening, and as this vision deepens even further within us, we will discover that our very essence is Love. As this realization matures, we will realize that our vision and essence are one and the same.

When we begin seeing and experiencing Life from this place of Unity—as Unity, so much of our life becomes uncomplicated. It does so because we are no longer seeing and meeting life from our egoic vision, which is inherently confused, divided and one sided. Because these two ways of perceiving are so radically different in how they view the world, one being fueled by ego and the other by love and unity, they will have a difficult time existing in the same room of our Self. The awakened vision will literally begin to destroy or break down our egoic way of seeing and being. It will simply because, the two will not be able to coexist together. One vision will have to give way to the other. If we are living as Unity, it will become too painful to hold a grudge against someone and see them as outside of our self. It will be difficult to get angry at our partner when we know that *we* are *them*. It will be difficult to argue with anyone's perspective or point of view, because we will see that all perspectives are false and based on conditioning. We will see that their perspective is human and we will finally, allow them to be as they are, without our ego asserting itself upon them. When we allow others to be as they are, without wanting to control or manipulate them in any fashion, our lives will become uncomplicated and we will begin to rest in the Unity and Mystery of this wonderful Life.

As this deepens within us, the very structure of our minds will begin to change. Our minds will begin to function differently. Our very way of perceiving reality will shift as our old or "normal" way of seeing the world breaks down. We will go through a disorienting period, perhaps over a number of years, when we are no longer perceiving the present moment as a projection of the past. In fact, our past memories and ability to remember may begin to dissolve as we begin to live in the fresh and alive present moment. As we look out on life we will see it as fresh and new, vibrant and alive, even if we are with old and familiar friends and in a familiar place. We will not relate to old friends in old ways, because our mind's perspective is no longer living in the past projections and is instead in the freshness of the present moment. What I am speaking about is not something that we are doing with our mind, like *trying* to be present. Rather, how the mind operates will shift from the old way of seeing and relating, and will begin to meet life from the present, fresh and direct experience of this moment. Many aspects of our lives will change as we step into this new way of being and relating to life. We may lose friends, discover new ones, spend great amounts of time alone, or transition to a new, more meaningful career; one thing is for certain, that our whole relationship to life will change as we step into this Divine Reality as our very own nature.

Many individuals on the spiritual path *try* to stay in the present moment. This usually involves some form of mental will power or efforting. What I am referring to is when the present moment comes and takes us by the neck, and radically reorients one's mind, so that it (our mind) can literally only function in the present moment. Not many people speak about this reorienting, but instead speak about living in "the now" as something we do or practice as some form of spiritual practice. Yet when enlightenment is a real movement within us, our energetic system within us gets rewired or rather, radically upgraded. It is easy for many individuals to speak about awakening from an intellectual perspective, and many can act like they are free, relying on their will power to maintain their freedom, but this is not the kind of freedom I am speaking about. I am speaking about surrendering and being taken by something much Greater than ourselves. True freedom is when Freedom comes and takes us and rewires our operating system so that we are in alignment with Freedom and have no choice about it. Adyashanti once said to me, that it was impossible for him to formulate a judgment and I wondered what he meant for years. Until one day, my mind began to have great difficulty forming judgments. I began to have trouble forming arguments for or against anything. I can remember many times, wanting to argue out of habit, but not even being able to form clear arguments in my mind about things that were once important to me. During this period, I was often at a loss for words and often found myself quietly confused because this aspect of my mind was no longer functioning within me. At times it was humorously pathetic to watch my mind feel emotional and want to argue, and yet my mind could not put together thoughts or memories to adequately support an argument. What I noticed also was that if people tried to argue with me, I couldn't even follow what they were saying, especially if they were deeply deluded. As a counselor, many times people have come to me with major complaints and arguments about life, and I kept noticing that I could not follow their delusion. What I began to see was that as soon as we are confused it means we are out of the world of

Reality. If we can become simple again, we quickly find our home in the Truth.

It is common that these judgmental and argumentative processes of mind begin to fall away in an individual over the years following a true awakening, and as these old processes fall away, the mind is reoriented in a way that sees unity and newness in every moment instead of seeing in terms of fear and division. This transition into unity consciousness opens the door to a whole array of different awakenings. It may even seem as if the entire universe is being destroyed and reborn in every moment. Our whole sense of time and the belief in the solid structure of the universe will begin to collapse as we awaken in this way. In our practical daily life, this experience can be humorous and even disorienting to the extent of being overwhelmed by a wonderful spaciousness as large as the universe and an intimacy akin to falling in love with every aspect of life. I have to laugh because for more than three years I have had the experience of each time I see my partner, I find myself again falling in love with her; it is as if I am seeing her for the first time. Ironically even if she is upset with me, I often am still falling in love with her, even in the difficult moments it is as if I am seeing her for the first time. And not only does this feeling of newness and love happen with her, it also does with most everything I come into contact with, whether it is my dog, a mountain, a river or a crowded subway car. As we become reoriented in this new way of being, our mind will begin to feel open, spacious and ever present and our being will radiate a causeless happiness. We may even have a difficult time remembering how we once lived in a way that was divided, tense and limited; and our whole way of perceiving life will shift from being defensive and fear based, to being relaxed and love based. As this shift happens, our very ability to get involved in conflict will greatly diminish. With the awakening of our hearts to Love as Love, we will go through periods of radical reorientation to life. We will find ourselves sometimes confused because we don't know how to relate to the delusion or insanity of the collective consciousness and instead we may find ourselves spellbound by the Beauty of tree or a mud puddle or an angry friend.

As this shift into Unity consciousness becomes more permanent and stable within us, we may discover deeper layers of our consciousness that are still lost in division and ignorance and we may find deep within ourselves these places that still view life through the lens of egoic defensiveness and division. Here we will again be invited to include and meet this aspect of our humanity with love and kindness, until it too is one day transformed. As long as we have a human body, we will have places within us that will be unconscious and will one day require our attention. The whole purpose of this world is for the growth and evolution of our expression of Divinity; to think that we will one day be done, complete or "totally" enlightened and no longer need to grow is pure arrogance. If we want to live in alignment with the Truth of this realm, with a beginner's mind, we go forward and lovingly embrace our opportunity to continually grow. No matter if we are stumbling in darkness or the brightest light on the planet, we are all growing.

Beyond working with the healing of *our* inner conflicts, the Divine will also invite us to begin to work on the level of the collective consciousness to heal and liberate the insanity of our collective consciousness that lives within us all. That being said, there really is no end to our work, and our work actually becomes the work of evolving our humanity on the collective level. As we give ourselves fully to this process and evolve more and more into a greater expression of Divinity, who and what we thought we were, becomes replaced by a causeless joy. We will radiate a movement of Divine force, which actively works and transmits through us, as Us and there will come a time when we will wonder how we could have ever imagined ourselves to be anything other than this force of Love on Earth.

About the Author

Craig Holliday is a Nondual Spiritual Teacher and therapist living in the mountains of Southwest Colorado. His work is dedicated to the discovery of our innate Divinity. He works in a way that addresses our everyday human suffering as a doorway to our inherent freedom. Craig offers Satsang, workshops, retreats and meets with individuals from around the world via Skype. For more information about Craig visit **craigholliday.com**

If you enjoyed this book please offer your review at the place of your purchase.

CPSIA information can be obtained at www.ICGtesting.com
Printed in the USA
LVOW08s1429240314

378692LV00001B/400/P